METRO MUSIC

Books by Gene Fowler

Border Radio

Crazy Water

Mystic Healers and Medicine Shows (Editor)

Mavericks

METRO MUSIC
CELEBRATING A CENTURY OF THE TRINITY RIVER GROOVE

GENE FOWLER & WILLIAM WILLIAMS

TCU Press
Fort Worth, Texas

Library of Congress Cataloging-in-Publication Data

Names: Fowler, Gene, 1950- author. | Williams, William Lewis, 1949- author.

Title: Metro music : celebrating a century of the Trinity River groove / Gene Fowler and William Williams.
Description: Fort Worth : TCU Press, [2021] | Includes index. | Summary: "Metro Music explores the musical history of Dallas, Fort Worth, and the surrounding area from the nineteenth century to the 1960s and the continuing echoes of that transformative decade. With nearly five hundred images, many previously unpublished, the book moves through genres and eras that include old-time fiddlers and string bands, singing cowboys, the blues, western swing, gospel, country-western, jazz, ragtime, big bands, Tejano and Tex-Mex, rhythm and blues, rockabilly, and rock 'n' roll"-- Provided by publisher.
Identifiers: LCCN 2020045935 | ISBN 9780875657714 (paperback)
Subjects: LCSH: Popular music--Texas--Dallas--History and criticism. | Popular music--Texas--Fort Worth--History and criticism. | Musicians--Texas--Pictorial works. | Dallas (Tex.)--Social life and customs--Pictorial works. | Fort Worth (Tex.)--Social life and customs--Pictorial works. | Badu, Erykah.
Classification: LCC ML3477.8.D35 F68 2021 | DDC 781.6409764/2812--dc23
LC record available at https://lccn.loc.gov/2020045935

TCU Box 298300
Fort Worth, Texas 76129

To order books: 1.800.826.8911

Design by Bill Brammer

COWBOYS

Came to the City Jail Singing

Medicine show songman Hunter Gassaway was killed crossing a Fort Worth street in 1945. As "lovable a character as ever the police ran in for drinking," Gassaway had "followed the medicine circuit since the turn of the century." He was "known throughout this area for his rich singing of the old South's songs, Negro spirituals, and folk ballads. On the little torch-lit stages in country towns he caught up his standing listeners with songs of Stephen Foster and the rollicking verses of levee toilers before the 'doctor' passed among them with the medicine bottles aloft. Police figure he had been arrested more than three hundred times in the last twenty-three years for drinking—just drinking. He never gave them 'trouble.' He came to the city jail singing and he sang in his cell to his cellmates. . . Carefree, impetuous and colorful, he liked to sing."

—*Fort Worth Star-Telegram*, April 26, 1945

Introduction

The Dallas-Fort Worth metroplex has a rich and storied musical history. The two cities and the small towns and rural areas around them have produced major artists and historic performances and recordings in just about every genre. And a diverse orchestra of voices continues those traditions today.

Fort Worth, the place where the West began long before Amon Carter coined the phrase, made important early contributions to the preservation of cowboy songs, and DFW artists like Michael Martin Murphey, Don Edwards, and Red Steagall played major roles in the genre's late twentieth-century revival. The dance halls, flour mills, and radio stations of Fort Worth gave birth to the "cowboy jazz" of western swing.

Texas country blues found a mecca in the streets and saloons of Dallas's Deep Ellum, attracting such important artists as Blind Lemon Jefferson and Leadbelly. Decades later, Dallas-born brothers Jimmie and Stevie Ray Vaughan, and many others from across the metroplex, helped popularize the ongoing blues revival. Likewise, a rebirth of the Deep Ellum neighborhood continues to showcase the eclectic range of sounds that embody Texas music today.

A handful of 1937 recordings by Robert Johnson at 508 Park in downtown Dallas marked a large patch of the cultural turf that sprouted 1960s rock 'n' roll. And if the brilliant producer and studio engineer Jim Beck, who recorded Lefty Frizzell and other landmark country-western artists at his Dallas recording studio in the 1950s, hadn't died at the age of thirty-nine, Big D—according to some—might have edged past Nashville as an industry center.

The eclectic range of sounds that embody Texas music today finds a voice in metroplex-launched artists as diverse as Erykah Badu, Leon Bridges, Norah Jones, St. Vincent, and Polyphonic Spree. And while many contemporary artists create surprising and unexpected sounds and styles, others offer a fresh but faithful take on just about every form from music's past.

Like all Texas music, the sounds created and enjoyed in Dallas-Fort Worth have historically been unique for the cultural melding of the region's three principal heritages: Anglo-European, African American, and Mexican American. And the independent streak bred into the Texas character has influenced the state's musical traditions, as well. Bill Boyd, for example, participated in singing cowboy, western swing, and country-western contexts and could have been included in any of the three. Sid Erwin spoke for many Texas artists when he remarked, late in his career, "I was too country for rock and too rock for country."

Harmolodics creator Ornette Coleman is said to have enjoyed jamming with western swing players. Big band singer Ella Mae Morse, an Anglo native of Mansfield, was often told, "You sing like a black girl." All across North Texas—urban, rural, small town—contemporary artists carry that rich heritage of mixed cultures with pride.

Metro Music is not intended to be encyclopedic in scope. Rather, the authors aim to represent genres and eras with images of bands and musicians both acclaimed and relatively unknown. While we regret the inevitable omission of any readers' favorites, there is always the allure of an encore.

We haven't been able to identify this mysterious and compelling fiddler, but he was photographed in Erath County circa 1939. Courtesy of Erath County Genealogical Society.

CHAPTER ONE

Fiddlers and Early String Bands

No Home Will Seem Perfect without a Guitar, Mandolin, or Banjo

When pioneers came to the province, republic, or state of Texas, whether for adventure, settlement, or to escape some misfortune or misdeed back east, if they were musically inclined, their saddlebags, wagon, or steamer trunk often carried a fiddle. The Devil's Box, as the instrument was sometimes called, was smaller than other instruments and easily transportable.

Former US Congressman David Crockett, for instance, may have played a Devil's Box in San Antonio after arriving there in 1836, perhaps even in the Alamo in the days leading up to the famous battle. Historians often dispute the notion, but self-proclaimed Alamo survivor Madam Candelaria told her audiences that "Crockett played the fiddle and he played it well, if I am any judge of music."

In 1843, Henry Journeay may have played a violin in a Mexican prison to entertain fellow survivors of the Mier Expedition. He reportedly built the instrument using pieces of glass, a razor, and wood scraps from a chair that had been made for Santa Anna. The Texas State Library and Archives occasionally exhibits the violin.

When botanic physician Gideon Lincecum arrived in Texas in 1848, his fiddle performance at a campsite picnic even entertained a pair of Native Americans encountered on the trail.

While none of these musicians settled in North Texas, the pioneer metroplex area was thick with fiddlers nonetheless. Kentucky native Dr. A. A. Johnston, for example, who came to Dallas in 1856, was reputed to be the "best old-time fiddler in the settlement." By 1900, when April showers stretched fiddle strings during one day of the Old-Time Fiddlers' Carnival held at the State Fair Grounds in Dallas, dozens of North Texas fiddlers convened to render their best versions of "Natchez Under the Hill," "The Big-Footed Mule," "Hell Broke Loose in Georgia," "Soapsuds Over the Fence," "Drunkard's Lament," "Old Gray Mare Came Tearing Out of the Wilderness," "Fisher's Hornpipe," and other chestnuts tried and true.

One scribe covering the event declared that carnival emcee J. T. Trezevant "knows and can tell you of the sentiment of the heart, the soul, which lies behind the querulous, quivering notes which, all strung out in a row, make up that almost heavenly inspired tune known as the 'Arkansas Traveler.'"

"In these days when the violin is played by musicians with classical educations and names that sound like a combination of a hay fever sneeze and the noise produced by tearing a clapboard off a smokehouse," ventured another correspondent, "the soul of a lover of melody who has been so fortunate as to escape a musical education yearns after the old, old tunes that bring back the days when the white-headed, gingercake-complexioned uncle fiddled in the corner."

Prizes awarded fiddlers included plover hams, gold watches, sets of harness, silver flasks, railroad tickets, cigars, and bottles of whiskey and beer. A performance of "Possum Up a Gum Stump" won one fiddler a silk umbrella. Judges included Governor Joseph Sayers, several sitting jurists, a minister, the aforementioned Dr. A. A. Johnston, and metroplex movers and shakers A. H. Belo and B. B. Paddock.

Judge George N. Aldredge waxed eloquent in his letter accepting an invitation to join the panel of appraisers. "I am a connoisseur of this kind of music," he wrote. "I well remember when in kilts, how my little soul floated in a sea of bliss as my ears drank the ravishing sounds that come from rosin and horse hair irritating the 'innards' of a cat . . .I would jump a ten-rail fence to get away from Paderewski, but I would walk a mile in the rain to hear 'Old Folks at Home,' 'Cotton-Eyed Joe,' or 'Mollie Put the Kettle On' by an old-time fiddler."

A fiddle contest held the next year, 1901, over in Cowtown led to the founding of an Old Fiddlers' Association. Henry C. Gilliland of Parker County won first overall prize, a gold watch, plus best "Dixie" and best "Arkansaw Traveler." Gilliland is regarded by historians as one of the first two musicians to record a commercially produced country music recording, recorded in New York in 1922 with fellow Texas fiddler Eck Robertson. In the Cowtown contest J.K.P. Harris of Granbury was deemed the most handsome fiddler. Additional prizes were awarded for oldest and whitest hair, tallest fiddler, ugliest fiddler, largest foot, oldest violin, longest beard, baldest head, and best Rebel yell. Moses J. Bonner of Fort Worth won for smallest foot and shortest fiddler.

Enthusiasm for the old-time fiddle tunes had not dimmed a generation later. On January 4, 1923, North Texans tuned the dials of their crystal sets, Radiolas, and Atwater Kents to Fort Worth's WBAP to hear Moses J. Bonner lead what may have been the nation's first radio barn dance broadcast. A five-piece string band called Fred Wagner's Hilo Five Hawaiian Orchestra, which normally only played Hawaiian music, accompanied Bonner on tunes like "Sallie Goodin" and "Yearling in the Canebrake" as Charles Rutledge called out the square dance moves.

The young radio station received more phone calls and telegrams about the hillbilly program than any of its broadcasts of pop, sacred, jazz, or semiclassical music. Two months later, Bonner

A longtime resident of Weatherford and Mineral Wells, Sam Savage used fiddle music to salve his memories of being abducted by Indians as a boy. Courtesy of Michael Lee Garrett.

W. B. Chenoweth, leader of the Chenoweth Cornfield Symphony Orchestra, was not only a fiddler but also an inventor whose creations included a machine that could purportedly extract electricity from the air. In addition to the Cornfield Symphony, he recorded as the Texas Fiddlin' Wampus Cat. Courtesy of Joseph Thomas Chenoweth.

Fiddlers pose on the steps of the Carnegie Library (now the Layland Museum) in Cleburne circa 1906. Henry Gilliland is the second fiddler from the far right. The man with the megaphone is "Doc" Smith, proprietor of the King-K Medicine Company, who sold his products at medicine shows throughout North Texas. Doc's great-grandson, Ronny Sterling, played bass with The Pendulums and The Jackals. Courtesy of Patricia Smith Boatright Collection.

took to WBAP's airwaves again on a bill with the Peacock Fiddle Band from Cleburne. (The National Barn Dance program did not serenade the ether on Chicago's WLS until 1924, and the Grand Ole Opry debuted on Nashville's WSM in 1925.)

The Chenoweth Cornfield Symphony Orchestra, a family string band led by fiddler W. B. Chenoweth, became one of the first ensembles to record not only in Dallas but in all of Texas when they waxed "The Last Shot Got Him" and "Hot Foot Step And Fetch It" for OKeh in November 1924. In addition to his status as a recording pioneer, W. B., who sometimes recorded under the name The Texas Fiddlin' Wampus Cat, was also an inventor. His 1946 obituary noted that "he claimed invention of the first six-cylinder automobile in 1899, a flying machine in 1908, a farm tractor controlled from the plow like a mule, and a machine for extracting electricity from the air."

In 1907, according to a TxDOT publication, he received the state's first automotive license plate for his six-cylinder, chain-driven, fourteen-passenger stagecoach motor bus, which operated a twenty-eight-mile route between Colorado City and Snyder. Still, his inventions never reaped the rewards they likely deserved, and the Wampus Cat was also known as the Moneyless Millionaire as early as 1912.

This virtual forest of fiddlers actively sawing away on their Devil's Boxes in the early days of Dallas-Fort Worth, however, does not mean that more classical fare, or even popular music played on other instruments, was completely neglected in pioneer North Texas. According to a 2014 *Oak Cliff Advocate* article by Gayla Brooks, the members of La Réunion, a short-lived utopian community established in Dallas in the mid-1850s, "were the first bona fide musicians in Dallas, possibly in North Texas. They arrived with small instruments but also brought an organ and a piano. Singing and dancing were part of the colony's routine, along with other cultural activities that lured Dallasites to the events."

Moses J. Bonner joined other fiddlers in a 1901 Fort Worth contest. When Bonner died at age ninety-two in 1939, his obituary said the Confederate veteran had been taught to fiddle by an elderly African American in Dallas. Courtesy of University of Texas at Arlington Special Collections.

LOCAL ARTISTS TO MAKE PHONOGRAPH RECORDS FRIDAY

For the first time in history, phonograph records for nationwide distribution, are to be made in Dallas by local artists.

This is to be made possible by a portable recording machine that will be brought here by the recording engineer of the General Phonograph corporation, makers of Okeh records. Will J. Schnelle, manager of the Texas Radio Sales company and local distributor for the Okeh records, made arrangements to have the machine brought here.

Jack Gardner's orchestra and Chenoweth's Cornfield Symphony orchestra are among those who will make the records. The recordings are scheduled for Friday.

In November 1924, the Chenoweth Cornfield Symphony Orchestra became some of the first musicians to record in all of Texas. Courtesy of Joseph Thomas Chenoweth.

Three Members of Cornfield Symphony Orchestra Play for Photogranler

The director and two of the other members of the "Cornfield Symphony Orchestra" are shown here. W. B. Chenoweth, the director, is standing. Thomas Chenoweth is playing the guitar and Joseph Chenoweth, 9 year of age, the banjo. Others in the orchestra, all of whom are members of the Chenoweth family, are Mrs. T. E. McGraw, pianist, and Mrs. E. J. Hayes, banjoist.

The Cornfield Symphony Orchestra included several Chenoweth family members. Courtesy of Joseph Thomas Chenoweth.

THE NEW ORLEANS ITEM

Southland Champions

The south's champion fiddler, W. CHENOWETH [illegible] [illegible]OE are playing this week at the Strand theatre.

W. B. Chenoweth on fiddle, Joe Chenoweth on banjo. Courtesy of Joseph Thomas Chenoweth.

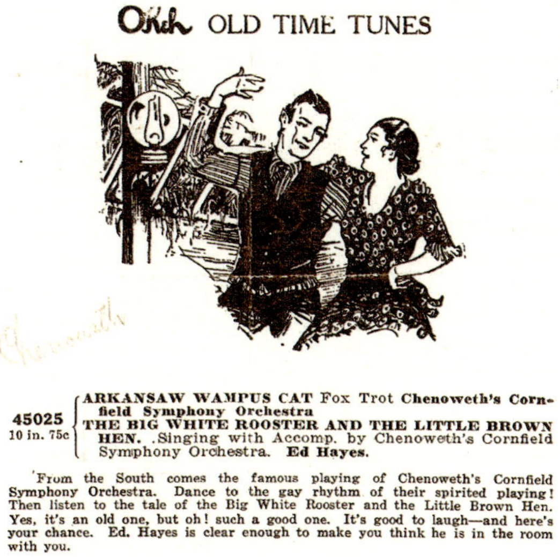

"Yes it's an old one but oh! such a good one." Early ad for Cornfield Symphony records on the OKeh label. Courtesy of Joseph Thomas Chenoweth.

Nor was fiddle or string band repertoire uniformly confined to old-time or hillbilly selections, as demonstrated by Fort Worth's Waldo Quintette, which may have been a subgroup of the Panther City Mandolin Club. In a report on Fort Worth musical talent published in the *Galveston Daily News* of August 31, 1896, the quintet's solo mandolinist Roy Simpson noted that the Waldo instrumentation included two mandolins, a mandola, one mandocello, and a lone guitar. The Waldo repertoire featured such selections as "Fra Diavolo" by Auber and Verdi's "Aida." Simpson also editorialized on the instrumentation of his group. "The mandolin, guitar, and banjo, much abused instruments, are rapidly coming to the front and will soon cease to be instruments of torture. The mandolin and guitar have made wonderful strides in the past few years and ere the coming season is over no home will seem perfect without a guitar, mandolin or banjo."

Fort Worth's Waldo Quintette, part of the popular "mandolin club" movement of the late nineteenth and early twentieth centuries, played classical fare. Seated left to right, unknown, Hatcher James, "Blinkie" (John) Trimble; standing, from left, Thomas P. Marlin and Malcolm Moore. Courtesy of University of Texas at Arlington Special Collections.

The student musicians in the Johnson School Fiddle Band, photographed in Stephenville in 1904, may not look terribly enthusiastic, but their outfits make up for it. Courtesy of the Stephenville Historic House Museum.

WAXAHACHIE DAILY LIGHT THURSDAY AFTERNOON

Pythian Home Musicians to Appear Here Friday

Pythian Home Mandolin Orchestra
Weatherford, Texas.

In the 1920s and '30s, Weatherford's Pythian Home for Widows and Orphans sponsored a Girls' Mandolin Orchestra that performed on Fort Worth's WBAP and throughout North Texas. For a time, the home also featured a harmonica band for boys. Courtesy of Bill McClung.

In the late nineteenth and early twentieth centuries, every town, it seemed, had their own string band. These fine musicians enriched the lives of folks in Cleburne. Courtesy of Michael Lee Garrett.

The Humphries Brothers (left to right: John, Jess, Cecil, and Olin). Reportedly, they once backed Leonard Slye, the artist who became known as Roy Rogers. Courtesy of Linda Jo and Scott Barker Collection. Photo by Swartz, Fort Worth.

Noted breakdown fiddler with a penchant for the blues, Prince Albert Hunt is shown here in military apparel circa 1921. Born in Terrell in 1896, Hunt performed with Chief Wahoo's Medicine Show and was, in his own words, "drunker than a hoot owl" during his recording sessions of tunes like "Blues in a Bottle," "Wake Up, Jacob," and "Traveling Man." Hunt was shot to death in 1931 by the estranged husband of his female companion outside the Confederate Dance Hall in Dallas. Courtesy of Marshall Wyatt and Old Hat Records.

Prince Albert Hunt is seen here with a guitar and two of his brothers. Courtesy of Marshall Wyatt.

This 1930 image of fiddlers and other musicians includes a young Bob Wills, first row, second from right. Guitarist Herman Arnspiger is second from right, second row. The photograph was likely taken sometime shortly before the formation and first radio performances of the Light Crust Doughboys. The handwritten caption on the image identifies it as "The largest fiddle band that ever played at one time. We all played 'Turkey in the Straw.' This picture was taken at night on Houston Street, Fort Worth, Texas." Courtesy of Carolyn Wills.

Based in Dallas in the 1980s, Randy Erwin captivated North Texas with his interpretations of classic cowboys songs, as well as his yodeling and rope tricks. Courtesy of Randy Erwin.

CHAPTER TWO

Singing Cowboys

Horse Rhythm

The cowboy singers in Fort Worth's White Elephant Saloon were not getting anywhere near the Ediphone recording contraption that John Avery Lomax hauled into the barroom—then located in the 300 block of Main Street—one night in 1908. Lomax had hoped to record them singing "The Old Chisholm Trail" and other songs. "I told the professor," said one hombre to his brethren, "that the Old Chisholm Trail Song was as long as the trail from Texas to Montana. I can sing eighty-nine verses myself. Some of the verses would burn up his old horn, and anyhow, I'm not goin' to poke my face up to his blamed old horn and sing."

As he wrote in his 1947 memoir, *Adventures of a Ballad Hunter*, Lomax did succeed in convincing at least one of the galoots to intone the tune, though not for his recording device. He had better luck with a gypsy fortune-teller camped on the West Fork of the Trinity. The "professor" was guided to her tent by her partner in charm, a young, handsome fellow who had disguised himself as a blind, elderly busker in the Stockyards, singing "doleful ditties" and listening "for the ring of quarters in his tin cup."

"To me," said the gypsy after singing the song about the Chisholm, "that is the loveliest of all cowboy songs. Like others, its rhythm comes from the movement of a horse."

Texas Christian University physics professor Newton Gaines, who performed cowboy songs and conducted scholarship on the genre, agreed with the gypsy. "The rhythms of the songs have been devised—probably quite unconsciously—to fit the gaits of the horse," said the physics whiz in a February 1941 news story carried in the

Newton Gaines, TCU physics professor and singing cowboy, poses on the porch of his Fort Worth home. Born in 1890, he learned cowboy songs at his uncle's ranch near Marfa. In addition to his scholarly articles on cowboy songs, Professor Gaines also published research on the effectiveness of sound waves in killing bacteria. In 1940 he recorded thirty Texas folk songs for John Lomax's collection in the Library of Congress. Courtesy of University of Texas at Arlington Special Collections.

Paducah Post, the *Saint Jo Tribune*, and many other Texas papers.

Dr. Gaines identified three gaits—the walk, the trot, and the lope—that produced the rhythm of most cowboy songs. "The real cowboy had to use horse rhythm in his singing," the professor remarked in 1947. "He had to sing to the motion of his horse, or get the breath knocked out of

Jules Verne Allen on tour, a rare example of an early singing cowboy with corporate sponsorship. Courtesy of the Albuquerque Museum.

him." Gaines began his own collecting of cowboy ballads at the age of nine. John Avery Lomax recorded him performing Western songs in 1911 and again in 1940. Lomax "always regretted that he couldn't sing," Gaines recalled, "but he was a splendid yodeler."

By the middle of the twentieth century, after the public had been immersed for decades in cowboy songs heard on the radio, on recordings, and on the silver screen, sagebrush classics like "Home on the Range" and "Streets of Laredo" seemed so engrained in American DNA that they must have been wafting in the wind when the Puritans landed at Plymouth Rock and Spaniards first crossed the Rio Grande. But it was the pioneering curatorial work of song collectors like Lomax and N. Howard "Jack" Thorp that rounded up these lyrics, tunes, and stories and preserved them for American culture.

It's been widely reported that Dallas and Fort Worth radio stations broadcast the first singing cowboy program when Stuart Hamblen took to the airwaves of WBAP and WFAA as Cowboy Joe in 1926. By 1929 Hamblen had rambled off to Camden, New Jersey, where—the legend says—he camped out in the lobby of Victor Records for a week with his dog Shep until the executives gave him a recording contract. He later found work in Tinseltown shoot-em-ups and became the first cowboy singer to record for Decca.

Jules Verne Allen billed himself on WFAA as the Original Singing Cowboy and later warbled on San Antonio radio as Longhorn Luke. Born in Waxahachie in 1883, his biography maintains that he began punching cattle in Jack County at the tender age of ten. "It's rather remarkable that the cowboy of fiction and movie fame," Allen opined in his 1933 book, *Cowboy Lore*, "does everything except caring for cattle."

That same year, the official Singing Cowboy

This page from a souvenir WFAA booklet includes, along with Peg, a photo of popular radio artist Ted Graves, who appears in cowgirl duds on p. 133 and uptown attire on p. 105. Courtesy of George Gimarc.

This portrait of Peg Moreland appeared in the *Cass County Sun* in 1927, indicating the singer's wide audience on WFAA. Courtesy of the Portal to Texas and the Atlanta, Texas Public Library.

of the Old Trail Drivers Association began a program on WBAP, *Jules Verne Allen's Cowhands*, that was geared to younger listeners. Fans of the program, which featured Old West tales and lore, along with "the genuine Plains ballads that have made Allen famous from coast to coast," could join the Cowhand Club and perhaps even meet the singer at a chuckwagon dinner "in the true Western style."

One Dale Evans poured her smooth pop vocals into the microphones of WFAA's *Early Birds* program for a time before hooking up with Roy Rogers. Another popular singer had a longer run on Dallas radio. "When the plaintive drone of *Bury Me Not on the Lone Prairie-e-e* is sailing over the ether and out of the speakers of thousands of sets in the Southwest it is a pretty safe bet that J. A. 'Peg' Moreland is at the business end of the microphone of WFAA, the Dallas News–Sears Roebuck station," reported the *Cass County Sun* on August 23, 1927. "Moreland regards the microphone as the campfire and the unseen radio audiences as his buddies gathered around it after a hard day on the range."

The "Cowboy Bard" and "Barnyard Tenor" told the scribe that his below-the-knee wooden stump was acquired when he "got kinda tired punchin' cattle" and tried "herdin' boxcars for a change" as a railroad brakeman. Said to know more than a thousand songs, Peg was also heralded as the beloved "King of the Ditty Singers."

In 1932, when Moreland broadcast for a brief time on the powerful Mexican border station XEPN in Piedras Negras, publicity from the station's Eagle Pass offices described him as "an old stage driver who croons the ditties of the camps and the songs of the trail." Whether he actually piloted stagecoaches or not will probably never be known, but another singer who started out on Dallas radio, Marc Williams, is perhaps even more mysterious.

Though Williams recorded many standards such as "Sam Bass," "The Cowboy's Dream," "When the Work's All Done This Fall," and "Little Joe the Wrangler" in the late 1920s and the 1930s, Douglas B. Green—a.k.a. Ranger Doug of the popular group Riders in the Sky—observed in his 2002 book *Singing in the Saddle* that Williams's "story remains shrouded in mystery . . . he rides into the history of the singing cowboy and out again as though in a snowstorm, leaving hardly a trace." Indeed, a 2004 reissue of his

Ellis County native Marc Williams performed on early Dallas radio and in person throughout North Texas as the "Cowboy Crooner." He later became a well-known children's entertainer as "Happy Hank" on Midwest radio and TV before retraining as a lawyer and returning to DFW. The singer is buried in Midlothian. Courtesy of Scott Tanner.

Don Edwards is widely regarded as "America's leading cowboy balladeer." Courtesy of Don and Kathy Edwards.

recordings is entitled *Marc Williams: The Forgotten Singing Cowboy*.

It is known, however, that Williams was born in Ellis County in 1903. He reportedly cowboyed as a young man and studied for a legal career before landing a gig as the Cowboy Crooner on KRLD from 1927 to 1930. He performed throughout North Texas and spent some time on the vaudeville circuit. In 1940, he reportedly parked his spurs for a spell on Fort Worth's KFJZ and appeared as Happy Hank on a children's radio program until at least 1947.

"Williams possessed a smooth singing style that contrasted sharply with the roughhewn sound of early cowboy singers such as Jules Verne Allen," wrote Kevin S. Fontenot in *The Handbook of Texas Music*. After his career took him to other parts of the country, he returned to Fort Worth in 1971, where he died three years later. His final bunkhouse is in Midlothian.

Don Edwards, widely regarded as "America's leading cowboy balladeer," headed west to the Fort Worth area in the 1950s. Born in New Jersey in 1939, the son of a former vaudeville magician, Edwards grew up enchanted by the West he found in Will James's books and in the music of Tioga, Texas, native Gene Autry.

Working on ranches, "chasing the rodeo," and playing a long-term gig at Fort Worth's venerable White Elephant Saloon, Don found the big state to be all that he'd imagined. In 1961, when Six Flags Over Texas held auditions for a cowboy singer/actor/stuntman, he won the job with renditions of two classics, "The Strawberry Roan" and "Cattle Call."

In 1997, Don followed childhood idols Tom Mix and Ken Maynard onto the silver screen, appearing in *The Horse Whisperer* as Robert Redford's singing sidekick, Smokey. That same year, he recorded a live Gene Autry tribute album at Autry's ninetieth birthday party.

After hearing his father sing cowboy songs at

With hits like "Lone Star Beer and Bob Wills Music," Red Steagall could easily have also landed in the chapters on country-western and western swing music. Courtesy of Red Steagall.

their home in Sanford, on the Canadian River, three-year-old Red Steagall enthralled his family audience by learning to warble the classic tune, "When the Work's All Done This Fall," in 1941. Overcoming childhood polio, Steagall regained the use of his fingers by playing mandolin and guitar, building up his strength by concentrating on one finger at a time. The very first song he wrote, "Here We Go Again," was recorded by Ray Charles in 1966. After writing hundreds of songs, Red got the cowboy poetry bug in 1985 when he attended the first National Cowboy Poetry Gathering in Elko, Nevada.

Steagall has hung his hat in Azle, northwest of Fort Worth, for some forty-plus years. And for thirty or so of those years, he has sponsored Cowtown's annual Red Steagall Cowboy Gathering and Western Swing Festival.

While growing up in the Oak Cliff section of Dallas in the 1960s, high schooler Michael Martin Murphey honed his artistry by performing at The Rubaiyat, a coffee house on McKinney Avenue. After recording some stellar albums during the "cosmic cowboy" era of the 1970s, he drilled down into cowboy music history and told his record label, Warner Brothers, that he wanted to do an album of classic cowboy songs. Company executives told the popular singer that such a move would be "career suicide."

But Murphey stuck to his guns, and the 1990 album *Cowboy Songs* went gold. As many Americans rediscovered the genre, Murphey explained to *Billboard* that the music of the West was "a very different animal" from country. "Country music is based upon the Appalachian culture," he told the magazine, "and we are based on the Mexican, black, and Scotch-Irish. There's also a heavy jazz influence on Western music, because when the big singing cowboy stars were popular in the '30s and '40s, that was also the jazz era."

Chuck Wagon crooner Lon Fishback had a long and varied music career in Fort Worth. Courtesy of University of Texas at Arlington Special Collections.

The first iteration of WBAP's Chuck Wagon Gang appears to have included popular songs, hymns, and cowboy songs on their programs, all delivered with Western flair. From left, the Gang is Piccolo Pete (Wylbert Brown), Little Joe (J. Villa Madin), Flapjack Jude (Julian Allen), and Big Joe (Lon Fishback). Big Joe was said to be "the only cowboy in captivity who wears his spats in wintertime and has never been astraddle a horse." Piccolo Pete, "the man with the talking fiddle, plays 'Pop Goes the Fiddle' on his head." Little Joe was reputed to be "the meanest and toughest man for his size in the whole gang," and Flapjack Jude lived in fear of "singing a high C and not being able to get down off of it." A 1935 report said that in their three years of performances, the outfit had sung over five thousand numbers. Gangster Wylbert Brown, oddly enough, owned the copyright to "The Eyes of Texas" for many years. Courtesy of University of Texas at Arlington Special Collections.

In 1930, while J. R. Hall was a student at Fort Worth's Polytechnic High School, he won a KTAT talent contest and was given a daily fifteen-minute radio show. Performing as the Utah Cowboy—even though he'd never visited Utah—he spent a couple of years in the mid-1930s performing on the powerful American stations XEPN and XELO in Piedras Negras, across the Rio Grande from Eagle Pass. After returning to Fort Worth, he continued his radio career on several metroplex stations until his radio retirement around 1948. Courtesy of Dolores McHargue and Doug Hall.

Popular singing cowboy and Tioga native Gene Autry at a personal appearance with the Dude Ranch Buckaroos in Big D circa 1947–48. Left to right: Louis Cook, Elmer Thompson, Autry, Cotton Whittington, Jumbo Drouin, Buzz Burnam. Courtesy of Kevin Coffey.

In 2016, Kristyn Harris, based in McKinney, Texas, became the youngest artist to receive the Western Music Association Entertainer of the Year award. In recent years, she has been performing with the Light Crust Doughboys. Courtesy of Kristyn Harris.

A. D. "Zuzu" Bollin, from Frisco, north of Dallas, was nicknamed after a popular ginger snap cookie. Seen here at what might be the Longhorn Ballroom (or Bob Wills Ranch House), Bollin was "rediscovered" late in life and enjoyed a career revival. As the debut release of the Dallas Blues Society, Chuck Nevitt produced Zuzu's *Texas Bluesman* album in 1989. Courtesy of Dallas Public Library.

CHAPTER THREE

Country Blues, Big City

Me and Lemon Gonna Ride on Down

A frequent sight in the Deep Ellum district of Dallas around 1925, which in those days included some bustling streets, buildings, and railroad tracks that were later pushed from the earth by the concrete march of Central Expressway, was a boy leading a blind man with a guitar and a tin cup. The boy was T-Bone Walker, who would grow up to introduce the electric guitar to blues music, and the man was the first country blues star, songster Blind Lemon Jefferson.

Born in Freestone County, Texas, around 1893, Jefferson is believed to have started performing in Deep Ellum around 1912. Blues researcher Alan Govenar has written that Jefferson "was known to perform almost daily at the corner of Elm Street and Central Avenue." Future Light Crust Doughboys pianist John "Knocky" Parker encountered Blind Lemon in Deep Ellum around 1922, when Parker accompanied his father there from their Ellis County cotton farm to recruit field workers. While his father searched for farmhands, Knocky, a four-year-old prodigy, played the piano in the African American district's Lone Star Saloon.

As Parker recalled to *Fort Worth Star-Telegram* writer Christopher Evans in 1984, one day when he was playing in the saloon, Blind Lemon walked in. "He asked somebody who was playin' that piano. I don't remember everything, but I remember how big he was. He came over and touched my face, felt my face all over to see who I was. And he felt of my hands. Then he got out his guitar, put it on his stomach and started playing. I tried to play everything on piano just like he did on guitar. . . . Lemon took me under his wing. He helped me learn."

The blind songster also shared the country blues with Huddie Ledbetter when the two musicians met in Deep Ellum around 1912. They often performed together in Dallas until 1915 (some sources say 1917), when Ledbetter—better known as Leadbelly—left Dallas. By 1918, Ledbetter had been returned to prison, convicted of murder. But during his time in Deep Ellum, the duo was so popular, Leadbelly said later, that "women would come running, Lord have mercy. They'd hug and kiss us so much we could hardly play."

Leadbelly recorded several tribute tunes to Blind Lemon. "Him and me was buddies," Leadbelly recalled during his final recording sessions in 1948. "Used to play all up and around Dallas-Fort Worth. In them times, we'd get on that Interurban line that runs from Waco to Dallas, Corsicana, Waxahachie, from Dallas. Then they had that Interurban that run from there to Fort Worth. We get out two guitars; we just ride." The busking duo often rode the line to a community called Silver City, described by Charles Wolfe and Kip Lornell in their 1999 biography, *The Life and Legend of Leadbelly*, as a rough suburb of Dallas. Leadbelly might have been referring to a Navarro

County hamlet by that name when he sang, "Me and Lemon gonna ride on down," in his song "Silver City Bound."

Reportedly, Leadbelly sometimes played mandolin or accordion during his performances with Jefferson. Blind Lemon would often play slide guitar with an open tuning, employing a bottleneck or a knife on the strings. Wolfe and Lornell note that Leadbelly would dance when Jefferson played a guitar solo on "Dallas Rag," a tune recorded years later by another Deep Ellum group, the Dallas String Band.

According to the 2013 volume, *Deep Ellum: The Other Side of Dallas* by Alan Govenar and Jay Brakefield, it was R. T. Ashford, the owner of a Deep Ellum shoeshine parlor and record shop, who convinced Paramount Records to record Blind Lemon in 1925. The 110 sides Jefferson recorded—including "Matchbox Blues," "See That My Grave Is Kept Clean," and "That Black Snake Moan"—were so well received, Wolfe and Lornell observed, that Lemon became "the nation's first real country blues star. His best-selling records would make him the most influential and popular of all the pioneer country blues singers, and Lemon's strange life and mysterious death in 1929 would make him the first of the great blues legends."

The swirl of legend and myth surrounding Blind Lemon Jefferson—and the strong association of Deep Ellum with African American culture—have led some to assume that the neighborhood's most enduring anthem, "Deep Ellum Blues," must be a Blind Lemon tune. Though Govenar and Brakefield cite anecdotal evidence that the popular song may have been performed in a bluesier style by black artists, the first of its many recordings was made in 1933 by an Anglo band called the Lone Star Cowboys.

Unsurprisingly, the sense of drama and danger one sometimes found in the neighborhood was somewhat exaggerated in the song's lyrics. Reports on Deep Ellum by journalists and historians can be similarly skewed. Still, accounts like *The WPA Dallas Guide and History*, compiled by Works Progress Administration researchers in the late 1930s, can give a sense of the area's flavor.

The *Guide* lists a variety of Deep Ellum businesses, including "secondhand clothing stores, job-lot emporiums, gun and locksmith shops, pawnshops, tattoo studios, barber shops, and drug stores." The Harlem Theater, at Elm and

Blues songster Blind Lemon Jefferson first appeared on the streets of Deep Ellum in the 1910s. Discovered by the owner of a shoeshine parlor and record shop in 1925, he went to Chicago to record for Paramount. Historians call him "the nation's first real country blues star." Blind Lemon's auditory powers were said to have been so keen that he could find his way through city and countryside by measuring the acoustic response to his guitar notes as the soundwaves encountered buildings, trees, etc. Courtesy of Marshall Wyatt and Old Hat Records.

Huddie Ledbetter, aka Lead Belly or Leadbelly, played on the streets of Deep Ellum with Blind Lemon, and the two rode the Interurban trains to perform in surrounding towns. Courtesy of Marshall Wyatt.

The earliest recording of "Deep Elm Blues" was by this group, the Lone Star Cowboys, in 1933. Left to right: Bob Attlesey, Joe Attlesey, Leon Chappelear. The Attlesey brothers had begun calling themselves the Shelton Brothers by the mid-1930s. Courtesy of Kevin Coffey.

Courtesy of George Gimarc.

Central, was "flanked by beer joints, cafes, domino halls, and the Gypsy Tea Room." The Indian Herb Store sold patent medicines, magic root powders, mojo bags, and good-luck charms in an exotic setting of stuffed creatures, Indian relics, and pickled medical displays. WPA researchers also visited the Wish-I-Wish Company on Central Avenue, purveyors of "love drops to attract the indifferent, magnetic lodestones for poker players, Van Van oil to shake a jinx, and High John the Conqueror lucky number root for general success."

The late Bill Neely, an Anglo country-bluesman in the Jimmie Rodgers style, whose repertoire included "Deep Ellum Blues," hitchhiked to Deep Ellum in the 1930s from his home in McKinney to listen and play at joints like Ma's Place. Neely remembered seeing "all kinds of people: cowboys, Mexicans, blacks, and down-and-out farmers, but what attracted me there was the music."

At the Tip Top, a tailor shop and dance hall, and at other spots, Neely and other Deep Ellum night crawlers could hear bluesmen like Lonnie Johnson, Little Hat Jones, and Funny Papa Smith. They could catch the hot sax of Henry "Buster" Smith and the jazz guitar of Charlie Christian, who drifted to Deep Ellum from Bonham. Jewell Nelson, Lillian Glinn, and Bobbie Cadillac elegantly moaned the blues. Whistlin' Alex Moore, Jesse Crump, and Texas Bill Day played the piano barrelhouse style.

Born in Dallas in 1899, Alex Moore first saw pianos in the homes of white customers to whom he delivered groceries along Ross Avenue. He plinked a key each time he saw one and slowly became familiar with the instrument. As he grew older he found easier access to a keyboard. In a 1982 interview, Moore told Alan Govenar that back in the 1920s "there was a piano in every shack in Deep Ellum, Elm Thicket [a black neighborhood near the Dallas Love Field Airport], and Froggy Bottom [near downtown Dallas and the Trinity River]."

Blues scholar Paul Oliver wrote that pianist Alex Moore spent most of his life in a small section of Dallas. "So his blues reflected a very personal, singular view of life, and because he is an eccentric man, his words are often unexpected and manifestly original." Courtesy of John Slate.

Blues scholar Paul Oliver and musicologist Chris Strachwitz recorded Moore for Arhoolie Records in 1960. "Alexander Moore had boundless ideas," wrote Oliver. "Betraying hardly a hint of influence from other singers, he played with great variety and sang in a throaty, husky voice. A man rich in worldly wisdom he was yet a man curiously limited in his knowledge of the world. Only once in his life had he left Texas; most of his life had been spent in a small section of Dallas. So, his blues reflected a very personal, singular view of life, and because he is an eccentric man, his words are often unexpected and manifestly original."

Courtesy of George Gimarc.

Coley Jones, another singular figure in Dallas's African American music scene of the 1920s, recorded eight songs with his Dallas String Band. Old-time music writer and 78 rpm record collector R. C. Montgomery describes the recordings on his weblog oldtimeblues.net as "incomparable to most anything else on shellac records." Coley Jones's repertoire ranged from ragtime to pop; none, Montgomery concludes, "could technically be classified as blues songs" but "bear some resemblance to white Texas string band music."

Marco Washington, who played bass with Jones's Dallas String Band, had a side project street band that included his wife and his stepson, Aaron Thibeaux "T-Bone" Walker. Aside from the family performances, Walker, whose earliest recordings bore the name "Oak Cliff T-Bone" for the Oak Cliff section of Dallas where he was raised, gained some of his earliest professional experience when, at age fifteen, he went briefly on the road with a medicine show selling Dr. Breeding's Big B Tonic (or B and B Tonic) when the show came through Oak Cliff.

"[The doctor] hired me and another boy, Josephus Cook, to ballyhoo for him," Walker recalls in the 1987 book *Stormy Monday: The T-Bone Walker Story* by Helen Oakley Dance. "[He] taught Seph and me to work up some patter about it and climb on the back of a panel truck to drum people in. I'd play and feed jokes to Seph, and he'd start in to dance. . . . Then we'd stack up the bottles, and Doc would come on. . . . The stuff he was selling was black and evil-tasting, but it brought the people out!"

Recorded in 1942 and released in 1945, "Mean Old World" has been called one of "the first important blues recordings on the electric guitar." Courtesy of George Gimarc.

Fort Worth Blues

In 1934, T-Bone was hired to lead the house band that played in the College Inn, a nightspot located in the lobby of Fort Worth's Jim Hotel. Built by the city's first black millionaire, William Madison "Gooseneck Bill" McDonald, in the late 1920s, the hotel was described by the African American newspaper the *San Antonio Register* in 1935 as "one of the most up-to-date colored hotels in the country. It has 62 bedrooms, a unique lobby, a commodious dining room with two individual mess rooms, a cozy general reception court and dance hall, a wine saloon, private bath and lavatories, etc. The building is one of hard-pressed red brick. The electrical fixtures and plumbing are designed in harmony of color. The furnishings from the bottom floor to the top are entirely new and modern." The Jim also became known as a fine venue for blues and jazz, one that drew touring and local white musicians in the wee hours after their own gigs.

T-Bone met his wife Vida Lee at the hotel. Born the youngest in a Waxahachie family of seven girls, Vida Lee came to Fort Worth after graduating high school. The girls' mother had died, and Vida Lee lived with an older, protective sister who felt that a twenty-four-year-old, charismatic blues musician was not the right match for such an innocent young girl. "I'd have had to be blind not to see how women shined up to that man," Vi told Walker's biographer Helen Oakley Dance.

His inquiries about her little sister rebuffed at first, T-Bone convinced the big sister to at least allow him to play cards with Vida Lee. "Then he started taking me to the picture show," she told Dance. It wasn't long before the couple eloped, and in 1936 they headed to Los Angeles, where T-Bone soon acquired his first electric guitar and introduced the instrument to the blues.

In other *San Antonio Register* reports, Sharps and Flats columnist Celeste Allen described the Jim Hotel as "the leading [African American nightclub] of the city" and "a favorite...fun spot." Another important blues venue, the Blue Bird, first offered musical entertainment sometime in the 1930s. Located in the Como neighborhood, an African American enclave on the west side of Fort Worth, the club was first located in a former trolley car, painted bright blue, from Como's defunct trolley line. "Around 1937," writes Michael H. Price in the 2018 book, *Fort Worth Jazz*, "Vastine and Viola Grant came to Como from East Texas, scrapped the streetcar, and built the present wood-frame structure, which they painted blue in a display of aesthetic consistency."

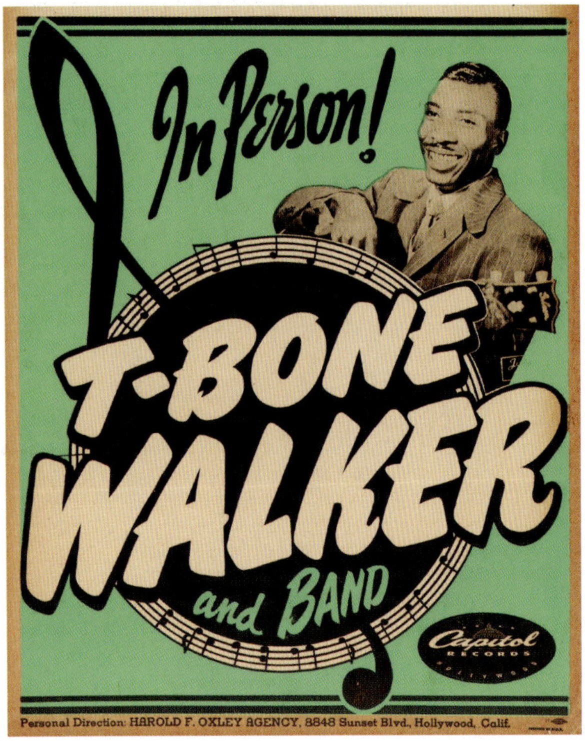

T-Bone Walker was popular in Dallas-Fort Worth, but his career really soared after he moved to Los Angeles in 1935 or 1936. Memories of his performances and his recordings continue to inspire Texas guitarists. Courtesy of George Gimarc.

The threat of the Trinity River overflowing its banks must have been a genuine concern for folks in Walker's Oak Cliff neighborhood. "That dirty Trinity River, sure have done me wrong / It came in my windows and doors, now all my things are gone." Recorded on 12-5-29, this was the B Side to Oak Cliff T- Bone's recording debut. Courtesy of George Gimarc.

Rose Room

Presents

THE ONE AND ONLY

T. BONE WALKER

AND

HIS ORCHESTRA

Sunday July 27 1947

Get Your Presale Tickets at Wards Ice Cream Bar, 2927 Thomas; Smith Drugs, Hall at Thomas.

Admission ---- $1.50

From 9:00 p. m. Until ?

For Reservation Call T-5913

All Star Floor Show Sat. Nite

Rose Room

Abe T. Salin & James F. Massoud, Owners

John Henry Branch, Mgr.

1710 Hall St. Dallas T-5913

In the 1940s, black artists performing at the Rose Room would sometimes play for white audiences at the Sylvan Club. Courtesy of Don O.

The New Blue Bird in the Como section of Fort Worth. Courtesy of Record Town, Fort Worth.

Bob Cooper's family reportedly started the first black taxi company in Fort Worth in 1917. In the '30s the Coopers acquired the Jim Hotel, a fifty-room hotel with a ballroom at 413 E. Fifth St. in downtown Fort Worth, where Bob became the night manager. The Jim featured legends such as Ray Charles, Sarah Vaughan, B. B. King, Fats Waller, and many others. In the '30s Cooper hired a young guitarist, Aaron Thibeaux "T-Bone" Walker, to lead the venue's house band. Courtesy of Sumter Bruton.

The musician who remains the most identified with the venue is Robert Ealey. Born in Texarkana in 1925, Ealey sang in church before moving to Dallas in his twenties. As Saturday night caught up with Sunday morning in his musical influences, he began singing the blues and drumming for other blues artists. And after relocating to Fort Worth, he formed the band Boogie Chillen with guitarist U. P. Wilson.

In 1976, when the Blue Bird's operator, Hiawatha "Shotgun" Gray, gave up the reins, Ealey took it over and rejuvenated it as the New Blue Bird Nite Club. Robert Ealey and his Five Careless Lovers—a mixed-race group playing for mixed-race audiences—became the putative house band. "He could sing any song in any key at any time," Careless Lover guitarist Sumter Bruton said after Ealey's death in 2001. "He made 'em up as he went along. He knew how the songs went, but you learned not to follow the words, because it was impossible."

Amongst his bag of vocal pyrotechnics, Ealey played air harmonica. "He'd put his hands up to his mouth, and it'd sound like he was playing a harmonica," said another Careless Lovers guitarist, Freddie Cisneros. "Then he'd take off on a scat,

The Blue Bird Club building when it was a taxi stand.
Courtesy of Record Town, Fort Worth.

U. P. Wilson played with Robert Ealey in The Boogie Chillen Boys. According to his 2004 obituary, he was known for a flamboyant style that included such tricks as placing his guitar flat on a table and playing it with one hand while he smoked or took a drink with the other. Courtesy of Don O.

Robert Ealey and his Five Careless Lovers at Mabel's Eat Shop, where one of the resident dogs was named Robert Johnson. Left to right: Rockin' Ralph Owens, Sumter Bruton, Robert Ealey, Freddie Cisneros, Jackie Newhouse (drummer Mike Buck unseen). Courtesy of Sumter Bruton.

and it wasn't like any scat I'd ever heard before."

Bill Minutaglio testified about a 1988 night at the Blue Bird—"the least stylish, maybe the best, blues club anywhere"—in his 2010 book, *In Search of the Blues*. "Time is frozen inside The Bluebird's fragile wooden walls. . . . The Bluebird is in a permanent state of decay, tilting toward the street. The bend in the building makes the booths look like a line of old-time roller coaster cars fading into a curve. . . . The Bluebird is the most integrated—racially and economically—club anywhere. On the dance floor, a 300-pound-plus man in overalls is rubbing a paw over his stubby beard and . . . gyrating with a blond woman in a black leather miniskirt and expensive-looking sweater. . . .Two burly guys in leather coats and cowboy hats are guffawing with two tiny women with beehive hair. Three yuppies are in a booth staring down at piles of barbecued meat they brought in from Red's Como Barbecue across the street. Alongside them, a 4-foot-high waiter is smiling down at the barbecue and applauding."

If those fragile walls inside the Blue Bird could talk, among the stories they could tell would be one of T-Bone Walker's final public performance. According to his *New York Times* obituary and other sources, his final show was a blues festival in Pittsburgh in late June 1974. But on the way back to Los Angeles, the bluesman stopped off in Fort Worth to visit his godson Nathan Lewis and other friends. And when he walked into the Blue Bird, Robert Ealey and his Five Careless Lovers broke into his theme song, "T-Bone Shuffle."

Walker sat in with the band on four numbers, including the signature "Stormy Monday." He played guitar on two of the songs and piano on the others. "His guitar style is a little shakier than it used to be . . . but it is still remarkably sensitive," wrote one observer in an unattributed clipping in Sumter Bruton's scrapbook. "His voice, always a strong point with Walker, is still mellow and full of life."

"Fort Worth is like my second home," T-Bone said to Pete Kendall of the *Fort Worth Press*. Sumter recalled that Walker spent several days in Fort Worth and also shared his weathered vocals for an intimate gathering at the home of Ornette's sister, Trudy Coleman. And Bruton and T-Bone spent some time listening to some of Walker's old 78s, especially the B-sides the younger guitarist hadn't heard, at Sumter's garage apartment. "I like that band," T-Bone told Kendall, speaking of the Careless Lovers. "Sumter comes closer to me than anyone, I believe. It makes you feel good to know there's still bands around Fort Worth like that."

The Blue Bird still stands today, ghostly and silent, as though the Careless Lovers or the Juke Jumpers will come back from a break and get the house movin' and moanin' with that lonesome thrill.

The Careless Lovers were, clockwise starting from lower left, Robert Ealey, Mike Buck, Sumter Bruton, Freddie Cisneros, Rockin' Ralph Owens, Jackie Newhouse. Courtesy of Mike Buck.

"I'm from Fort Worth, so I sing like I talk."

One night in 1966, a teenage guitarist from Dallas sat on the banks of Waller Creek, behind the Saracen Club on San Jacinto Street in Austin, holding his new Rickenbacker while Jimmie Vaughan played his black Les Paul. After demonstrating some B. B. King riffs he'd just learned, Jimmie expounded, "I'm telling you, man. The blues is where it's at. This stuff, B. B., Freddie, this is what I want to play."

Many of the musicians who sparked the Austin blues revival of the early 1970s drifted down to the capital city from Dallas and Fort Worth. They included singers Lou Ann Barton and Paul Ray, drummers Doyle Bramhall and Mike Buck, bass player Alex Napier, and guitarists Denny Freeman, Derek O'Brien, and the Vaughan brothers. "We all kind of lived out our dream of playing in a blues band," said Ray (1942-2016) in a 2014 interview. He'd grown up listening to blues artists who came through Dallas on the Chitlin' Circuit, and his band Paul Ray and the Cobras became one of the mainstays of Austin's

In addition to many other career highlights, drummer Linda Waring, seen here at the Cellar in Dallas, played with blues rockers Bugs Henderson, Johnny Nitzinger, and Rocky Hill. In 1969, Bob Sims wrote, "Linda is the percussion fan's Janis Joplin, hunched over her drums, making savage sounds and mumbling mysteries to herself like an alchemist turning lead to gold." Courtesy of Linda Waring.

Jackie Newhouse, Stephen Bruton, Mike Buck, and Sumter Bruton at The Hop in Fort Worth. Bob Dylan and Bonnie Raitt dropped by The Hop one night when Stephen Bruton was playing. Courtesy of Sumter Bruton.

Buddy Whittington lived in Richland Hills until age thirteen and has hung his hat in Hurst ever since. Here he is as a teenager. Courtesy of Buddy Whittington.

Buddy Whittington (left) toured with blues great John Mayall (right) and his Bluesbreakers from 1993 to 2008. Courtesy of Buddy Whittington.

Courtesy of Record Town, Fort Worth.

Fort Worth's James Hinkle described his music as "Eclec-Tex," or just Texas music. "There's some country, some Cajun, some Tejano, some rock, and some blues all mixed in there. A little bit of all the stuff in me." Courtesy of Don O.

The Juke Jumpers, seen here in 1981, formed in Fort Worth in 1977 "when Jim Colegrove and Sumter Bruton decided to form a band that played rhythm and blues, blues, jump and rockabilly in a traditional Texas style." Left to right: Michael Bartula, Jim Milan, Johnny Reno, Jim Colegrove, Sumter Bruton, Craig Simecheck. Courtesy of Jim Colegrove.

Lou Ann Barton and Alex Napier were two of the many artists who drifted down to Austin from the metroplex and helped establish the capital city's blues scene of the 1970s. Courtesy of Kathie May Hejny.

Denny Freeman, with Bubu Watson, maracas. Courtesy of Kathie May Hejny.

blues scene before vocal problems caused him to retire from singing.

Previewing a Jimmie Vaughan—Lou Ann Barton Aztec Theater bill in 2017, Hector Saldana wrote in the *San Antonio Express-News* that Barton "remains one of the greatest blues singers that Texas has ever produced."

"I'm from Fort Worth, so I sing like I talk," she told Saldana. "I sing blues with a country accent. I can't help it." *Austin Chronicle* writer Margaret Moser described Barton as a "sassy Fort Worth shouter who cut her teeth playing Jacksboro Highway juke joints" and a fashion trendsetter "with her wardrobe of torchy cocktail dresses and dangerously high heels." And Moser credited a *Rolling Stone* image of Lou Ann sitting on Muddy Waters's knee at the Austin blues club Antone's as the "enduring image" that put the city on the blues map.

Jimmie Vaughan had uncles who played guitar in country-western bands, and, like another standout Dallas guitarist, Seab Meador, he grew up idolizing English guitarists—and, of course, Jimi Hendrix, for a while. In 2010, he contrasted his style with that of his younger brother Stevie (1954-1990) for *Texas Monthly* writer Mike Shea: "I don't really think they were that different, except that I would try to play like B. B. King and Freddie King and he tried to play like Jimi Hendrix. . . . If he couldn't get over with an audience, he'd do Hendrix, and everybody's mouth would drop, so he sort of incorporated it into his style. He had to try harder 'cause he was a little kid."

"Say something with the notes."

Rolling Stone ranked Freddie King (1934-1976) the twenty-fifth all-time greatest guitarist on its 2003 list of the 100 greatest. The Gilmer native established his career in Chicago before settling in Dallas in 1963. Brandy Herbert, a younger guitar ace, treasures the memory of a unique apprenticeship with King. "It came about when Floyd Dakil and the Pit Men left the Pit Club, and the management put together a whole new band," Brandy remembers. "I was the lead guitarist, and John Anderson, I believe, was the general manager of The Pit. I was going on and on about Freddie King one day and, of course, like every guitar player in Dallas, I knew all the Freddie King instrumentals. And the manager said, 'Oh

Dallas-Fort Worth natives Alex Napier, Paul Ray, and Denny Freeman helped establish the "blues revival" in Austin during the "cosmic cowboy" era of the 1970s. "That's John Henry Alexander on drums," says Denny Freeman, "and Bubu Watson on maracas. Looks like Alexander's Place, a black bbq joint in what was then 'out in the country,' southwest of Austin. This is an early version of Paul Ray and the Cobras." Courtesy of Kathie May Hejny.

One of the first blues songs to be published, "Dallas Blues" was written and issued by an Oklahoma City music publisher in 1912. Courtesy of University of Texas at Arlington Special Collections.

Largest Circulation of Any Dallas Weekly
EVERY FRIDAY — 10,000 COPIES — FREE

SEPIA DALLAS

JULY 8 THRU JULY 14

B. B. KING who along with his SENSATIONAL 10 piece BAND will provide the MUSIC — YOU want to hear at the LONGHORN RANCH comes MONDAY, JULY 11th — TICKET — ah yes — you can get'm at the usual places.

Long before multiculturalism was cool, the Longhorn Ranch or Longhorn Ballroom was hosting blues artists like B. B. King, shown here in 1960. *Sepia* magazine began in Fort Worth in 1947 as *Negro Achievements.* After the death of its black publisher, Horace J. Blackwell, it moved to Dallas in 1951 and became *Sepia* under the sponsorship of white businessman George Levitan. Courtesy of George Gimarc.

Jimmie Vaughan, above and right, had uncles who played in country-western bands, and he started out himself in rock bands. But by the mid-1960s, he knew he wanted to play the blues. After playing in The Pendulums, The Chessmen, and other Dallas bands, he joined The Fabulous Thunderbirds in the '70s. Younger brother Stevie Ray followed suit. Both brothers' artistry amazed fellow musicians and music fans alike. Courtesy of Kathie May Hejny.

Courtesy of Donna Vaughan.

Stevie Ray Vaughan. Courtesy of Kathie May Hejny.

Robin Syler (foreground) and Tommy Shannon played together in the first iteration of Krackerjack. The band later included a teenaged Stevie Ray Vaughan, who played rhythm to Robin's leads. Dallas critic Tim Schuller wrote, "Mark me, few of the renowned guitarists on this planet are a tenth as good as Syler." Robin defied categories, deftly weaving Dick Dale-esque surf sounds into his blues. He also played pedal steel with Homer Henderson, toured with boogie kings Canned Heat, and played briefly with the Werewolves (often described as "Dallas' answer to *Exile on Main Street* Rolling Stones"). His bandmates in the Millionaires were Doyle Bramhall and Alex Napier. "Robin had an amazing feel," said Doyle. "He was always pushing the envelope on guitar. He could play just like Albert King, Albert Collins, or Hound Dog Taylor, but he didn't want to sound like anyone else, just like he didn't want to look like anybody else." Courtesy of Carol Galt.

yeah, Freddie is a good friend of mine.' I thought, Yeah right. He says 'No, would you like to meet him?' So he picks up the phone. 'Freddie, dude, got this kid here who really thinks you're hot shit.' Hands me the phone. Freddie King's on the other end of the phone. He says, 'So you're a fan, huh?' I said, 'Yeah, I know all your songs.' He says, 'Well, you want to come over some Sunday, we'll hang out.' Sounded good to me! So I went over to Freddie King's house at least a half dozen times, on a Sunday generally. His wife cooked up soul food. Mashed potatoes, greens, fried chicken. Freddie and I would sit down in the living room and work a little bit, she'd serve up a mess of food, and we'd go eat a little bit then come back and play some more.

"But Freddie really had an influence on me from the standpoint of my attitude towards the playing, of course, like every other kid back then. They call it shredding now, but we could play all these blues licks so fast. We knew the blues scales backwards and forwards. I could just rip that stuff off in my sleep. So I'd go over there and Freddie would say, 'Okay, I'm gonna play 12 bar blues, and you play something, then we'll switch it up, then you play 12 bar blues and I'll play something.' And we'd do that for a little bit, and Freddie says, 'Okay, you got speed, I'll give you that. Tell you what, I'm gonna play 12 bar blues, and you can play anything you want except you only get to use one finger of your left hand.' Okay, so now you have to stop and think about where you're coming from and where you're going to and how are you going to construct a real melody line, not just licks and riffs and pull-offs and hammer-ons and all that stupid lead guitar shit. I'm thinking, Okay fine, so I'd go home and work on that, and next week we'd come back and do it again. Then one week he said, 'Congratulations, you just graduated to two fingers!'

"Then over a space of the next three or four weeks I'd graduate to another finger, and like, all of a sudden, I really started thinking about what I'm playing. And to this day I can't play with that kind of speed I had when I was 18, 19. But I learned something more important. What I learned was I learned to say something with the notes. It's like it's more important to say something with the right ones than with the most ones, you know, which has always been B. B. King's thing. But Freddie was just a sweetheart. I just loved that man. He was a big influence on me."

The great Freddie King. DFW musicians say Freddie had an upstairs "office" at Mother Blues on Lemmon Ave., where he held court during all-night poker games. Below, sharing a bill with Delbert McClinton's early band, the Strait-Jackets. "You've got to *say something* with the notes," Freddie counseled younger guitarists. Courtesy of George Gimarc.

Courtesy of Record Town, Fort Worth.

The 1989 recording session for the Zuzu LP, *Texas Bluesman*. Left to right: Zuzu Bollin, Buster Smith, Doyle Bramhall, Sumter Bruton, Duke Robillard, Gerard Daily, Hash Brown. Courtesy of Sumter Bruton.

Zuzu Blues

Reminiscing about Fort Worth's Jim Hotel in 1991, saxophonist Leroy "Hog" Cooper—a former member of Ray Charles's band who grew up in Dallas—said to *Star-Telegram* writer Christopher Evans, "I started going to the Jim Hotel in the early 1950s, when (late, legendary Fort Worth saxophonists) King Curtis and Red Connor were hanging around. Then, when I got out of the Army in 1952, I went back to Texas and did a date at the Jim with a guitar man named Zuzu Bollin. I don't know whatever happened to him."

It's understandable that Cooper wondered what happened to Zuzu, for Bollin's story is one of those classic tales of a promising young artist who disappeared, dropped out of sight only to be rediscovered decades later for a brief career re-

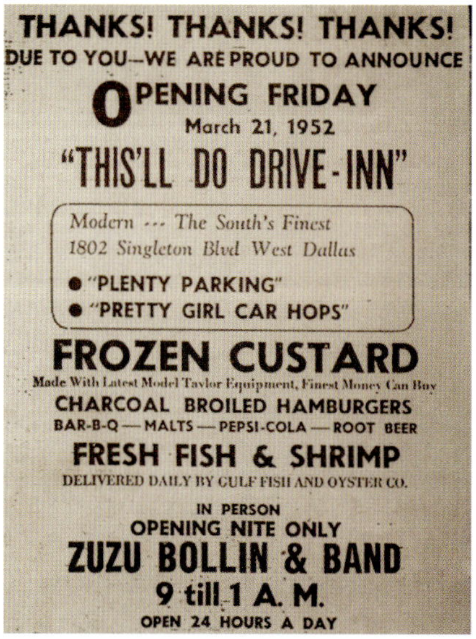

Courtesy of Trinity River Music.

vival late in life. Born in Frisco, north of Dallas, around 1923, Bollin grew up next door to a juke joint, where he was schooled by a jukebox of 78s by Blind Lemon and other blues performers, as well as big bands like Count Basie. When Bollin found his own musical voice, wrote blues historian Tim Schuller in a 1989 *D Magazine* story, his specialty became "'jump' blues, which mixed the emotionality of down-home blues with the citified sound of big-band swing."

Zuzu obtained his memorable first name from a brand of ginger snap cookies he fancied. His first recordings, on Dallas's Torch label in 1951, featured a band that included not only Leroy "Hog" Cooper on sax but David "Fathead" Newman, as well. Bollin's "Why Don't You Eat Where You Slept Last Night?" stood a good chance of becoming at least a regional hit, but Bollin maintained that Dallas nightclub owner Jack Ruby waged a campaign to keep it off local radio and jukeboxes. Reportedly, Ruby was miffed when Zuzu raised his booking fees after the record's initial splash.

A combination of factors caused Bollin's career to stall, and he faded from the scene, working for a time as a dry cleaner. When Dallas blues lover Chuck Nevitt tracked Zuzu down in 1987 at a rooming house, the bluesman had fallen on hard times. Nevitt talked him into attempting to get back in the groove, and as Schuller wrote, "The first place they hit was Fort Worth's Bluebird, the old-style blues bar with the ambience of a bait store. Zuzu took the stage with the band of U. P. Wilson, a guitarist who counts Zuzu as an influence, and let fly."

The Zuzu revival included a much-lauded new album, *Zuzu Bollin: Texas Bluesman*, and high-profile performances that included the Chicago Blues Festival and Holland's Blues Estafette. Sadly, Bollin's artistic resurrection was cut short in 1989, when he died of cancer.

Blind Lemon, Leadbelly, Zuzu . . . all the blues artists who played the streets and joints from Deep Ellum to the wide-open town where they say the West began . . . all would agree, we deeply believe, with the testimony of T-Bone Walker when asked about the music that juiced his soul. "The blues? Man, I didn't start playing the blues ever. That was in me before I was born. And I've been playing and living the blues ever since."

"There's blues in my rock and rock in my blues," sang Dallas-based guitar legend Bugs Henderson. Courtesy of James Anderson.

Raised in a musical family of East Texas sharecroppers, Melvin "Lil' Son" Jackson headed for Dallas as a young teen in the late 1920s. In Deep Ellum he heard some of the artists he'd listened to on recordings back home. He also formed a gospel group, the Blue Eagle Four, that played around town. After serving in World War II, he returned to Dallas and achieved some success with recordings, but a 1956 car wreck caused an early retirement from music. Working in an automobile scrapyard, he was "rediscovered" in 1960 by Chris Strachwitz, who recorded him for Arhoolie Records. Courtesy of Ted Tucker.

Born in Hughes Springs, Texas, in 1905, Babe Kyro Lemon "Black Ace" Turner is said to have built his first guitar himself. He later played a National Style 2 squareneck tricone that he fretted with a glass medicine bottle. By 1936, with tours and recordings under his belt, he had a radio show on KFJZ in Fort Worth. After his service in World War II, he reportedly did not return to music until 1960, when Chris Strachwitz visited him in Fort Worth and asked him to record for Arhoolie. Black Ace is seen here with Mrs. Turner at their Fort Worth home not long before his death in 1972. Photo by and courtesy of Freddie Cisneros.

Music was soaked into Lucky Peterson's genes while growing up in Buffalo, New York, where his musician father ran the Governors Inn, a regular stop for touring artists. Lucky started playing as early as age three, and Willie Dixon produced his first album when Lucky was an old-timer at age five. He reportedly appeared on such programs as *The Ed Sullivan Show* and *What's My Line?* as a child. In his teens he played guitar and keys with Etta James, Bobby "Blue" Bland, Little Milton, Otis Rush, and others. He first moved to Dallas in the late 1980s and returned again in 1996, remaining after marrying singer Tamara Stovall. The music community of the metroplex and beyond was shocked and saddened by his death in 2020 at age fifty-five. Courtesy of Don O.

Son of the late drummer Doyle Bramhall, Doyle II grew up around some of Texas's finest musicians. He has toured with, recorded with, and produced an eclectic array of gifted artists. He plays the guitar upside down and left-handed, bending the strings downward like Albert King. "It just felt comfortable to hold a righty guitar left handed, and it never occurred to me to change the strings." His professional career began by touring with The Fabulous Thunderbirds when he was eighteen. Playing acoustics and dobro, Doyle joined Eric Clapton for the historic "Sessions for Robert J" project at 508 Park Ave. in Dallas, where they recorded Robert Johnson's songs at the exact spot where Johnson recorded in 1937, including "Love in Vain" and "Hellhound on My Trail." Courtesy of Donna Vaughan.

Renowned big band leader Paul Whiteman, whose orchestra played an extensive run at Fort Worth's Frontier Centennial in 1936, is shown here with Blackie Simmons & His Blue Jackets on Cowtown's "Paul Whiteman Day." Left to right: Knocky Parker, accordion; Jimmy Brown, fiddle; Sam Graves, banjo; Bruce Pierce (later "Roscoe"), guitar; Whiteman, conducting; Blackie Simmons, fiddle. Whiteman leased the Van Zandt farm while in Fort Worth and went riding each day in a twelve-gallon hat and monogrammed chaps. He also kept up his weekly national radio show, broadcasting from the Ringside Club on the Jacksboro Highway. Courtesy of University of Texas at Arlington Special Collections.

CHAPTER FOUR

Western Swing

That Fort Worth Beat

The unique and delightfully semi-inscrutable musical brew called western swing percolated to life in the Depression-era house parties, dance halls, radio stations, and flour mills of Fort Worth. Tulsa musicologist Guy Logsdon noted that "it contains elements of many other musical forms such as pop, blues, jazz, Dixieland, traditional folk, fiddle, ragtime, and even an occasional touch of classical. Its origins are attempts to emulate big-band sounds on string instruments."

Retired Texas State University professor Gary Hartman, whose band Lone Star Swing helps keep the music alive in Central Texas, took a crack at defining the genre in his 2008 book, *The History of Texas Music*. "Western swing," he wrote, "is an eclectic blend of traditional fiddle breakdowns, country ballads, blues, ragtime, jazz, swing, pop, polkas, schottisches, and other musical styles."

The term western swing itself wasn't in widespread use until Spade Cooley adopted it to promote his sound in California in the 1940s. But as Cary Ginell explains in his 1994 book, *Milton Brown and the Founding of Western Swing*, it has since become synonymous with many Texas bands formed in the 1930s, including the Light Crust Doughboys and Brown's own Musical Brownies.

Fans still debate which seminal figure—Bob Wills or Milton Brown—played a greater role in the genre's development. According to Charles R. Townsend's 1974 biography, *San Antonio Rose: The Life and Music of Bob Wills*, the young fiddle player quit barbering in Turkey, Texas, in 1929 and headed for Cowtown. Fort Worth was full up on barbers, but Wills found a little work constructing the stage for a medicine show and then performed in the physic opera. He also went on the air at WBAP, but without a sponsor the broadcast could not put food on the fiddler's table.

At some point—probably around Christmas, 1929—Wills met vocalist Milton Brown and his guitar-banging younger brother Derwood Brown at a house dance. Bob Wills, Milton Brown, and guitarist Herman Arnspiger began playing together for dances and—as the Aladdin Laddies sponsored by Aladdin Lamps—on radio. Sometime in 1930, Burrus Mills sales manager W. Lee O'Daniel agreed to sponsor the group on radio programs advertising the Burrus product Light Crust Flour. The band's first broadcast was either in the fall of 1930 or early 1931. Before long, Derwood joined the group, and the Light Crust Doughboys became a quartet.

O'Daniel, who hated the group's "hillbilly" music, canceled the program after a few weeks. But when announcer Truett Kimzey showed the salesman the fat bags of fan mail the Doughboys had received, the savvy O'Daniel relented and put them back on the air. Sales of Light Crust Flour boomed.

The flour mogul turned into a big fan of hillbilly music and took over the Doughboys' announcing duties, insisting that the group play a homey, sentimental repertoire. Milton Brown helped the Burrus boss adapt the tune, "Just Because," which had been made popular by the Shelton Brothers, to accommodate words O'Daniel wrote for the syrupy anthem "Beautiful Texas."

One of the earliest photos of the Light Crust Doughboys, circa 1931. Left to right: Milton Brown, Derwood Brown, announcer Truett Kimzey, Bob Wills, Herman Arnspiger. Courtesy of Hill College W. R. Auvenshine Library Light Crust Doughboys Collection.

Conflicts arose between the wildly popular musicians and the stern sales manager, especially over the issue of the band playing dances. O'Daniel felt that an association with the "disreputable establishments" such as the Crystal Springs Dance Pavilion might harm the snow-white reputation of Light Crust Flour. Seeking artistic freedom, as much as for any other reason, Milton Brown left the Doughboys in September 1932.

Milton Brown and His Musical Brownies went on the air that same month. Bandleader Milton continued performing some of the tunes that made the Doughboys so popular, but he also added jazz, blues, and pop songs. North Texans flocked to Crystal Springs to dance to the Brownies every Saturday night. And when Milton added piano player Fred "Papa" Calhoun to the band in late fall of 1932, according to Cary Ginell, western swing was officially born.

Two years later, the Brownies pioneered the addition of steel guitar to a string band, adding Bob Dunn to the lineup. Dunn was reportedly the first musician to amplify a steel guitar. Waco fiddler Jimmy Thomason was one of thousands listening to the Doughboys and the Brownies on the radio. As he told Cary Ginell, "When I heard . . . that 'Milton Brown Beat,' as we called it, why that changed my entire outlook on music." Sadly, the charismatic bandleader Milton Brown died from injuries sustained in a 1936 car wreck on the Jacksboro Highway at the age of thirty-two.

Clashing with O'Daniel over the boss's demand that the band not play dances and over just about everything else, Bob Wills left the Doughboys a year after Milton Brown. Bill C. Malone, in his landmark *Country Music U.S.A.*, first published in 1968, attributed the split to a wage dispute. Wills's biographer Charles Townsend wrote that O'Daniel fired the fiddler because Wills's drinking had caused him to miss too many radio

Banjoist Marvin "Smokey" Montgomery joined the Doughboys in 1935, a year before posing with this mobile Photophone Sound Recording unit. Smokey remained a Doughboy until his death in 2001. Courtesy of Hill College W. R. Auvenshine Library Light Crust Doughboys Collection.

Before heading for Texas in the mid-1930s, Marvin Montgomery, seen here, at right, with his cousin Orville Dooley, performed in tent vaudeville around his native Ohio. Courtesy of Hill College W. R. Auvenshine Library Light Crust Doughboys Collection.

broadcasts. Whatever the case, Bob headed for Waco with his new group the Texas Playboys, the band long most associated with western swing. The group found greater success in Oklahoma, California, and eventually, back in Big D.

O'Daniel himself was fired by Burrus Mill in June 1935. The resourceful and ambitious businessman and media strategist promptly formed his own company, Hillbilly Flour, and his own promotional band, the Hillbilly Boys. His colorful flour sacks included a mountain goat, musical notes, and a four-line ditty about the product: "HILLBILLY music 'on the air' / HILLBILLY Flour everywhere; / It tickles your feet – it tickles your tongue, / Wherever you go, It's [sic] Praises are sung." And right below the verse appeared the slogan O'Daniel made famous: "Please Pass the Biscuits, Pappy."

In 1938, when "Pappy" O'Daniel decided to jump into politics with a long-shot campaign for governor of Texas, he stumped the state with the Hillbilly Boys. "They've come to town with their guitars / And now they're smoking big cigars / Them hillbillies are politicians now," the Boys sang in one of Pappy's gubernatorial compositions. Relying on his media stardom to win the governor's race, O'Daniel proved to be an erratic public servant. When Texas radio stations demanded advance copies of his increasingly peculiar and politically partisan speeches, Pappy sidestepped the mainstream media by becoming part owner of a powerful radio station that blasted its signal northward from Reynosa, Tamaulipas. The governor of Texas addressed his constituents from an electronic communications outpost in a foreign country.

Hillbilly music on the campaign trail proved just as popular in a special US Senate election in 1941, when the Hillbilly Boys helped catapult Pappy to national office, in the process handing Lyndon Johnson the only electoral defeat of his career. But O'Daniel proved just as ineffective a senator as he had governor. As one Pappy fan put it, "I've been listening to W. Lee O'Daniel on the radio for many years, and he's a good man. It ain't his fault he didn't do nothin'."

Dallas Morning News columnist Lynn Landrum seemed more concerned with whether the Hillbilly Boys and their leader were genuine hillbillies. "How many of the flour-barrel Hill-Billies know . . . the taste of cold spring water out of a gourd dipper from a cedar bucket? How many ever saw hominy corn hulled, with lye taken from the drip-

The Doughboys, 1935. Left to right: Raymond DeArman, Leon Huff, Hubert Barham, Eddie Dunn, Clifford Gross, Kenneth Pitts, Doc Eastwood. Courtesy of Kevin Coffey.

kettle under the ash-hopper trough? How many of them know a good coon dawg when they see one? . . . If Texas needs Hill-Billies to . . . restore gubernatorial prestige, then, by all the varmint hides nailed on the smokehouse door, Texas is entitled, to shore-'nough Hill-Billies. If these flour-barrel boys are mere drugstore imitations, the sooner we tear away their mummers' masks, the better."

The revolving cast of Hillbilly Boys band members were given cutesy nicknames invented by Papa Hillbilly himself. Vocalist Leon Huff was the Texas Songbird. Guitarist June Whalin was dubbed Jerry the Love Bird, while fiddler Carroll Hubbard was introduced as Little Caesar, the Fiddle Teaser. When vocalist Kitty Williamson joined, Pappy swooned over Texas Rose. O'Daniel's sons Pat and Mike, who began taking music lessons when the biscuit baron realized the marketing mojo of hillbilly music, eventually joined the band as Patty Boy and Mickey Wickey.

The band's sentimental and upbeat repertoire included the official O'Daniel campaign theme, "Please Pass the Biscuits, Pappy," which lifted its melody from the popular "I Like Mountain Music." In the O'Daniel composition, "My Million Dollar Smile," the Hillbilly vocalist sang that he'd "said skidoo to hard time blues." Other bands paid tribute to the flour power phenomenon, as well, including the Bar X Cowboys of Houston, who released the Pappy tribute, "Bluebonnet Governor." In 1938, Gene Autry was set to star as O'Daniel in Republic Pictures's Hillbilly Governor, but the production was derailed.

Other politicians noted the Pappy campaign model. When Texas land commissioner Jerry Sadler entered the 1940 gubernatorial contest against O'Daniel, he campaigned with his own band, Sadler's Cowboy Stringsters. And when LBJ ran unsuccessfully against Pappy for the US Senate in 1941, he took a cue from the flour mogul, campaigning with an all-out patriotic revue featuring a six-piece (non-hillbilly) swing band and songstress Sophie Parker, billed as the "Kate Smith of the South." In his successful 1948 campaign, Johnson opted for a more down-home ensemble, as Miss Cleo and the Texas Farmhands, led by accordionist Cleo Raymond, played for some of his rallies.

We don't know where this costumed lineup of the 1933 Doughboys was headed, but we're sure it was a grand occasion of big fun. That's W. Lee O'Daniel at the microphone. Left to right: Clifford Gross, Sleepy Johnson, Leon Huff, Herman Arnspiger, O'Daniel, Raymond DeArman, Leon McAuliffe. Courtesy of Kevin Coffey.

The Musical Brownies in the studios of Fort Worth station KTAT. Likely circa fall of '32. Top row, left to right: Jesse Ashlock, Milton Brown, Wanna Coffman. Bottom, left to right: Ocie Stockard, Derwood Brown. Courtesy of Ted Tucker.

"In flour it's the protein that counts," but on the radio it's that hot hillbilly jazz. Courtesy of Kevin Coffey.

Seen here in Hollywood in 1936, the Doughboys could really swing when they played from the back of this beauty. Note the radio station lineup. Left to right: Zeke Campbell, Clifford Gross, Dick Reinhart, Bert Dodson, Marvin Montgomery, Kenneth Pitts, Eddie Dunn. The woman is probably Kay Hughes, and the guy in the white suit at far right is Smiley Burnette. Courtesy of George Gimarc.

Milton Brown's Musical Brownies, seen here in 1937, continued for a time after the popular singer's death in 1936. Left to right: Lefty Perkins, Mike Gallagher (announcer), Derwood Brown, Wanna Coffman, Buck Buchanan, Johnnie Borowski, Fred Calhoun, Ocie Stockard. Courtesy of Kevin Coffey.

Cuttin' a rug and mixing with the musicians during World War II at Crystal Springs Dance Pavilion. Musicians include Johnny Crawford, sax/clarinet; Homer Kinnaird, drums; Derwood Brown, guitar; Wanna Coffman, bass; George Bell, piano; and Jimmy Brown, fiddle. Courtesy of Ted Tucker.

Courtesy of Kevin Coffey.

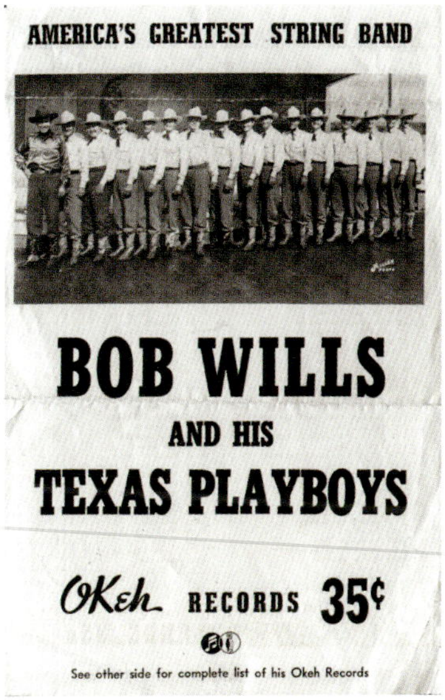

After leaving the Doughboys in 1933, Bob Wills founded the Texas Playboys and then moved to Waco and Oklahoma, where he began to find the success that established him, to many fans, as the King of Western Swing. Courtesy of Ted Tucker.

Crystal Springs Ramblers, left to right: Buck Buchanan, Jerry Robinson, John Lee Sparks, Earl Driver, Papa Sam, Henry Cunningham, Jimmy McAdoo, Myrle Barber, Jerry Byler. Courtesy of University of Texas at Arlington Special Collections.

Along with the Musical Brownies, the Crystal Springs Ramblers were mainstays at Papa Sam Cunningham's wildly popular Crystal Springs Dance Pavilion in Fort Worth. Top, left to right: Morris Deason, Earl Driver, Jimmy McAdoo, Ebb Gray, Joe Holley. Bottom, left to right: Papa Sam and Henry Cunningham, Loran Mitchell. Circa 1937. Courtesy of Kevin Coffey.

When O'Daniel founded his own flour company, Hillbilly Flour, in 1935, he also started his own band, the Hillbilly Boys. The band was not only effective at selling flour but also at getting votes when Pappy ran for governor in 1938 and senator in 1941. Here's the gang at Fort Worth radio station KGKO in 1938. Left to right: Kitty Williamson, Bundy Bratcher, Wallace Griffin, Leon Huff, Mike O'Daniel, Kermit Whalin, W. Lee O'Daniel, Pat O'Daniel, Molly O'Daniel. Courtesy of University of Texas at Arlington Special Collections.

O'Daniel and the Hillbilly boys at a rally in 1939. O'Daniel at microphone, Curley Perrin in the lighter shirt with guitar, flanked by Leon Huff and Bundy Bratcher. Courtesy of University of Texas at Arlington Special Collections.

Texas school children of the late '30s and early '40s learned Pappy O'Daniel's sentimental state song by heart. A couple of lines of the song appeared in his 1939 gubernatorial inauguration booklet. Courtesy of Trinity River Music.

"They've come to town with their guitars..." Courtesy of Trinity River Music.

Twin fiddles, Bob Wills (right) and Johnny Strawn (left). Courtesy of Phil Strawn.

Vocalist Ramona Reed joined Wills in late 1950 and stayed til '52, when this photo was taken at the Bob Wills Ranch House. Standing, left to right: Al Turner, Skeeter Elkin, Joe Andrews, Eldon Shamblin, Bob White, Joe Holley, Ocie Stockard, Paul McGhee, Luke Wills. Seated: Ramona Reed and Bob Wills. Courtesy of David Dennard.

The Temple of Western Swing

Bob Wills moved back to the metroplex in 1950, when Big D's most thankful millionaire O. L. Nelms built the western swing maestro a Texas-sized honky tonk at the corner of Cadiz and Industrial, south of downtown Dallas. Something of a prototype for today's Billy Bob's in Fort Worth's Stockyards, Bob Wills Ranch House was big as a football field—maybe bigger—and the wall-to-wall cowboy kitsch included a bar inlaid with 1,700 silver dollars. Indoor stalls provided parking space for horses, and Wills occasionally rode his steed Punkin, outfitted with special rubber shoes, out onto the dance floor.

For the grand opening on November 15, advertising shouted that the "Show Place of the Nation" would be celebrated with a "big parade" at noon, featuring, in addition to Bob and the Boys, "visiting governors, stars of radio, stage, and screen," and stars from the Madison Square Garden—Dublin, Texas Rodeo, along with "trick ropers." A 10 p.m. to midnight TV broadcast on WFAA carried the proceedings throughout the Dallas-Fort Worth area. Weeks later, ads proclaimed Wills the "granddaddy of western swing."

The "voluble" Jack Ruby, as one newspaper wag described the Dallas nightclub operator, kept the name Bob Wills Ranch House when he took over the sprawling joint in 1952. Ruby assumed emcee duties at the Ranch House, camping it up in Western duds as he introduced Tex Ritter, Ernest Tubb, and T. Texas Tyler.

Dewey Groom acquired the Ranch House in 1958, renamed it the Longhorn Ballroom, and operated the club through New Year's Eve of

At Panther Hall around 1966. From left to right: Jerry Case, guitar; Leon Rausch, vocals and bass; Jimmy Belken, fiddle; Bob Wills, bandleader and fiddle; Jerry Howard, drums; Johnny Manson, fiddle; Phil Sperbeck, pedal steel. Courtesy of Johnny Case.

1985. Growing up in Van Zandt County, Groom had traded a bull calf to acquire his first guitar. He came to Dallas in 1936 at the age of eighteen, playing guitar and singing for customers as he pumped gas at a filling station. Eventually, according to his 1997 obituary in the *Dallas Morning News*, he became a partner with Jack Ruby in two nightclubs, the Top Rail and the Silver Spur, also performing at the clubs.

Groom parted ways with Ruby, he said, because Ruby didn't like his countrified clientele. "He wanted to make it an elite Western club," Groom explained. Ruby didn't like it that people wore jeans and even overalls to the venue. "He was running 'em off faster than I could run 'em in." But, added Groom, "I made him money. He was starving to death when I first met him. We built the place up to turn-away crowds."

Free from the pesky neuroses of Jack Ruby, Groom guided the Longhorn Ballroom into a long, sunny run that was uncommon in the world of live music joints. He led an eleven-piece house band, Dewey Groom and the Texas Longhorns; recorded for the Longhorn Records label; and in that monument built to western swing he booked everyone from Hank Thompson, Willie Nelson, and Loretta Lynn to Nat King Cole and the Red Hot Chili Peppers.

In 2020, the temple built for western swing was up for sale, occasionally filled with music and laughter some seventy years after its stage was first graced by Bob Wills and his Texas Playboys.

When rockabilly and rock 'n' roll started crowding big bands off the jukeboxes in the 1950s, Wills was quoted in the press, "Rock and Roll? Why, man, that's the same kind of music we've been playin' since 1928! . . . But it's just basic rhythm and has gone by a lot of different names in my time. It's the same, whether you just follow a drum beat like in Africa or surround it with a lot of instruments. The rhythm's what's important."

Yes ma'am, that Fort Worth beat.

Popular Dallas honky-tonk man and western swing bandleader Dewey Groom bought the Longhorn Ballroom from wheeler-dealer O. L. Nelms and ran the immense dance hall for many years. Front row, left to right: Billy Chambers, Buddy Brady, Billy McBay, Bob Shirey, Groom, Clay Allen, George McCoy, Bobby Garrett. Back row, left to right: Freddy Dawson, Phillip Sanchez, Bob Monroe. Courtesy of Steve Bonner.

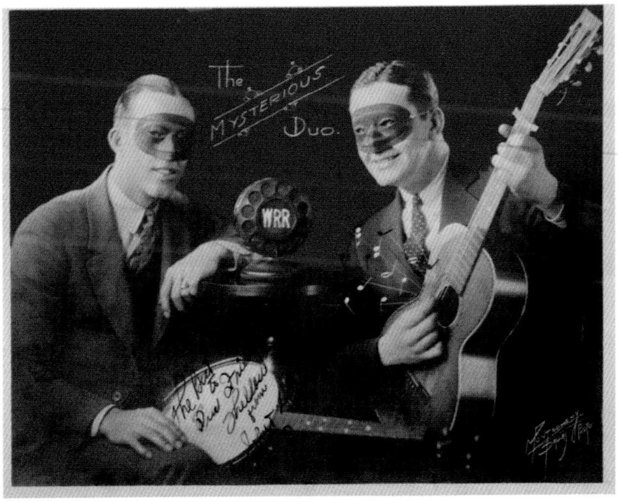

The Mysterious Duo of Dallas station WRR in the mid-1920s consisted of staff musicians Roy Newman (on right) and John Thorwald. The musicians pretended to be exiled Russian noblemen, who had to disguise their identity to avoid Russian guerrillas. Press reports said the duo could yodel "with the most royal blood in the land, and can play the guitar and piano and sing with any dictators living today." Newman went on to lead a series of important western swing bands, which included such metroplex players as Dick Reinhart, Jim Boyd, and Alfredo Casares. Courtesy of George Gimarc.

Before his death in 1941, a third brother, John Boyd, played steel guitar with the Ramblers. Randall "Buddy" Neal, guitar; John Boyd, steel; Gar Austin, fiddle; Bill at mic, Ish Erwin, and Jim Boyd. Courtesy of George Gimarc.

Art Guinn's western swing band at the Aragon Ballroom in Dallas, circa 1969. Left to right: back row, Art Guinn, Casey Dickens, Jesse Harris, Johnny Case, Dick Bridges, Walter Lyons. Front row, George Uptmor, Judy Beaver, Ted Lynch, unidentified. Courtesy of Johnny Case.

Born in Fannin County in 1910, Bill Boyd, at microphone, and his brother Jim, second from right, performed on Greenville Station KFPM as teenagers. After moving to Dallas, Bill played on Jimmie Rodgers's 1932 Big D recording session. His western swing outfit, Bill Boyd and His Cowboy Ramblers, enjoyed a long radio and recording career. Jim played with the Doughboys, the Crazy Gang, and his own Men of the West. Left to right: Cleo Hoyt, Fred Casares, Bill Boyd, Jim Boyd, Ken Lasater. Courtesy of Kevin Coffey.

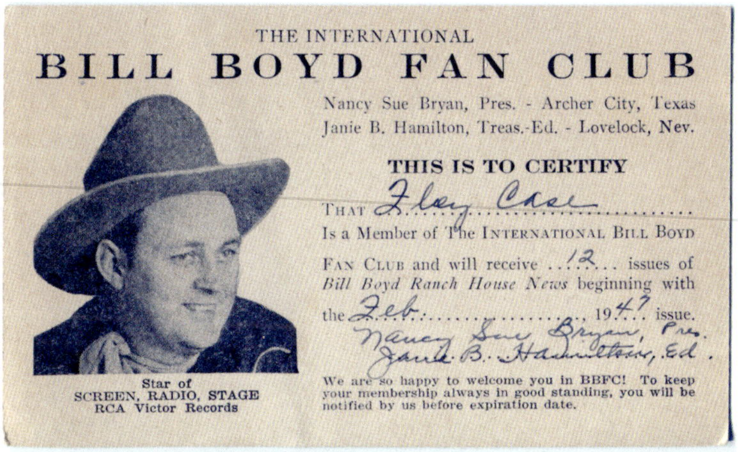

THE INTERNATIONAL

BILL BOYD FAN CLUB

Nancy Sue Bryan, Pres. - Archer City, Texas
Janie B. Hamilton, Treas.-Ed. - Lovelock, Nev.

THIS IS TO CERTIFY

THAT Floy Case
Is a Member of The INTERNATIONAL BILL BOYD FAN CLUB and will receive 12 issues of *Bill Boyd Ranch House News* beginning with the Feb. 1947 issue.

Nancy Sue Bryan, Pres.
Janie B. Hamilton, Ed.

We are so happy to welcome you in BBFC! To keep your membership always in good standing, you will be notified by us before expiration date.

Star of
SCREEN, RADIO, STAGE
RCA Victor Records

Pioneering country music journalist Floy Case was also a Bill Boyd friend and fan. Courtesy of Johnny Case.

Bird-Brand Shortening had its own Western Swing/Cowboy Music advertising ensemble, the Bird-Brand Cowboys, led by Slomie—a.k.a. Buck, a.k.a. Jack—Creel. In the large group photo, the boys are visiting Waco. Shown are: Hi Pockets Castleman, guitar; Liston Weaver, bass; Cyclone Burgess, tenor banjo; Uncle Jim Castleman, fiddle; Buck Creel, accordion. And the Bird-Brand Pan-Americans brought Latin spice to the program. Courtesy of George Gimarc.

Courtesy of George Gimarc.

Courtesy of George Gimarc.

"Next stop Waxahachie," says Homer Zeke Clemons on his 1950 Imperial recording "Dallas Limited," where "sweet potatoes grow in the sandy land, where every family has ten children and every child has a twin." Left to right: Dub Dickerson, Homer Zeke Clemons, Joe Rea, Tiger Echols, Red Mullins, Ken Lasater. Courtesy of Kevin Coffey.

Oliver "Sock" Underwood grew up in Hearne, a fan of the Musical Brownies. He got his nickname from playing high school football. Heading for Cowtown in 1936, he eventually joined the Crystal Springs Ramblers and founded his own band in 1950, which featured a musical adventurousness that accommodated sit-in performances by Fort Worth jazz great Ornette Coleman. As Maria Golia notes in her 2020 book, *Ornette Coleman: The Territory and the Adventure*, Underwood loved jamming with black musicians because they seemed more open-minded about western swing than most white jazz artists, many of whom looked down their noses at the "hillbillies." Left to right: Buddy Wallis, mandolin; Billy Briggs, tenor sax; Gene Crabb, drums; Louis Cook, bass; Sock, guitar. Courtesy of Kevin Coffey.

Like the Brownies, Roy and his Boys dressed sharp in big-city suits, 1937. Left to right: Top row, Ish Erwin, Bob Dunn, Cecil Brower, Jim Boyd, Charlie Lockhart. Middle row, Randall Neal, Thurman Neal, Holly Horton, Earl Brown, Walter Kirkes. Bottom row, Harry Sorensen, announcer, and Roy Newman. Courtesy of Kevin Coffey.

In 1947, *Billboard* reported receipt of the latest souvenir booklet for Slim McDonald's "new, modernistic bistro," Dallas's Ole Top Rail, where "entertainment is in the hands of Patty Lou and Her Texas Sweethearts." Courtesy of George Gimarc.

DFW radio stations in the '30s and '40s often featured all-female western swing bands, and the gals could also slow it down for an effective range ballad. The Texas Cowgirls at KGKO in Fort Worth, 1940. Left to right: "Bess" (Ruth Mulkey), "Sue" (Gail Whitney), "Sally" (Ruth Murphree), "Marge" (Veda Mae Spoon), "Bertie" (Bertie Evelyn Keisel). Courtesy of George Gimarc.

The father of rockabilly legend Ronnie Dawson, Pinkie Dawson led the western swing house band at Dallas's Manhattan Club, which was near the still-standing Sons of Hermann Hall in Deep Ellum, circa 1938-39. Seated left to right: Bill Vitovsky, possibly George Thomas, Lowell Horton. Standing left to right: Aldan Hutson, two men from the Manhattan Club management, Leaford Hall, Aubrey Gass, Jimmie Smith, Mack Register, Pinkie Dawson. Courtesy of Kevin Coffey.

A longtime western swing favorite, Louise Rowe was still performing a regular gig in Euless as Louise Rowe and the Texan Playboys in the 2010s. Fiddler Jimmy Belken at left. Courtesy of Johnny Case.

Sponsored by Fort Worth's Universal Mills, the Universal Cowboys were a varied-repertoire staple on DFW radio in 1938 and '39. "When you visit the Texas State Fair at Dallas on Tuesday, Thursday, or Saturday, be sure to see the 'Universal Cowboys' as they present their noonday program from KGKO's studios in the Automobile Building....the boys invite you to stop by and get acquainted." Circa late 1938. Left to right: Steve Wooden, Lefty Perkins, Clifford Gross, Charlie Willhoite, Dick Reinhart, Doc Eastwood, Darrell Kirkpatrick. Courtesy of Kevin Coffey.

Those good old days when furniture stores sponsored their own western swing ensembles. Left to right: Warren Harrison, fiddle; Speck Bradley, tenor sax; Jack Hinson, piano; Ross Aldridge, manager; Aldan Hutson, guitar; Raymond Littlejohn, bass; Rankin Moulder, tenor banjo. Courtesy of Kevin Coffey.

The postwar HiFlyers, after a brief Del Rio sojourn with the big border station XERA. Left to right: Elmer Scarborough, Zeke Campbell, unidentified woman, Grady Maples (announcer), Teddy Anderson, Jerry Byler, Billyevan Gober, Andy Schroder. Courtesy of Kevin Coffey.

The Flying X Ranchboys appeared on the first "official" broadcast of Amon Carter's WBAP-TV in 1948, and their program remained one of the station's most popular in its early years. Left to right: Lefty Perkins (who played a right-handed guitar left-handed), Mel Cox, Marvin Montgomery, Bruce "Roscoe" Pierce, Red Kidwell, Carroll Hubbard. Courtesy of Kevin Coffey.

"There's nothing fancy about these boys but their socks," said a 1940 news article about the Sunshine Boys. "Turnip Greens" was cited as the Boys' anthem, and other popular tunes included "I'll Be Seeing You in Dallas, Alice." The Boys (left to right) are Merle Shelton, guitar; Billy Mack, steel guitar; Bob Shelton, behind Billy Mack; Slim Harbert, bass; Jimmy Thomason, fiddle; Bruce Pierce, banjo, "doubles on hog calling"; Joe Shelton, mandolin. Courtesy of the University of Texas at Arlington Special Collections.

Lookin' Starlighter-sharp here, George Petton played guitar with Bob Wills, in addition to his work with the Western Starlighters. Courtesy of Deborah Petton Bell.

The Western Starlighters, circa late 1950s. Left to right: George Petton, Bob Wallin Charlie Meeks, Gary Van, Billy Braddy, Pee Wee Wharton (front), Ken Crabtree, Red Watson. Courtesy of Deborah Petton Bell.

Western Starlighters. Charlie Meeks, kneeling left; Pee Wee Wharton, kneeling right; Gary Van, standing right. Courtesy of Deborah Petton Bell.

Steel guitar ace Billy Braddy wore the distinctive Starlighter chapeau for a spell. Courtesy of Deborah Petton Bell.

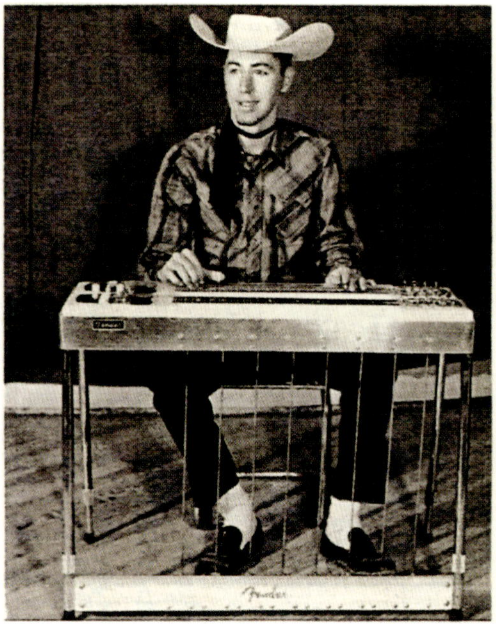

Described by Steel Guitar Forum as "a cantankerous character who didn't suffer fools," Tom Morrell was a brilliant steel player, western swing and otherwise. Also a Starlighter for a time, he played on recordings for Asleep at the Wheel, Talking Heads, and Don Edwards, in addition to his own band, the Time Warp Top Hands. Courtesy of Johnny Case.

Denny Mathis, 1963, shortly after joining Billy Gray's band.
Courtesy of Johnny Case.

Fort Worth accordionist Ginny Mac has taught classes on western swing at TCU. She discovered the instrument when she saw an accordion player at Eagle Mountain Elementary at age seven. Then as a young teen she discovered a new world of musical expression at Cowtown Opry's Texas Heritage Music Program in the Fort Worth Stockyards. "My teacher, Devon Dawson, introduced me to 1930s and '40s Western swing bands that used a lot of accordion," she explains. Ginny is shown here in 2019 performing with her brother, Glenn McLaughlin, at Webb Gallery in Waxahachie. A multi-genre artist and multi-instrumentalist, Glenn's studies have included classical guitar, gypsy jazz, and swing. He has taught at the Bobby Boatright Western Swing Music Camp and other schools and has shared stages with the Texas Playboys, Asleep at the Wheel, Hot Club of Cowtown, and many others. Courtesy of Ginny Mac / photo by Lewis Lee.

Years before their mega-popularity as a transformational country band, The Chicks were a dynamic western swing and cowgirl ensemble based in DFW and known as the Dixie Chicks. Here, sisters Martie and Emily Erwin flank former Chick Laura Lynch when the group performed at Bill Clinton's first presidential inauguration in 1993. Courtesy of Laura Lynch.

The seven-piece band Shoot Low Sheriff keeps western swing alive in DFW today. Courtesy of Shoot Low Sheriff.

The 2015 version of the Light Crust Doughboys performing at the State Fair of Texas. Left to right: Marek Eneti, Jim Baker, Dion Pride, Art Greenhaw, Randy Wills. Photo by Misti Pierce. Still going in 2020, the ninety-year-old band seemed on track to hit one hundred. Courtesy of Art Greenhaw.

Fort Worth journalist Bob Ray Sanders said that Francine Morrison had "a soulful, deep-rooted gospel voice that could touch the heart and sting the soul." Courtesy of Black Academy of Arts and Letters, Dallas.

CHAPTER FIVE

Gospel

God Can Be Cool

"When I'm singin', I'm prayin'," said Fort Worth gospel artist Francine Morrison in 1984. "I try to touch people's spiritual side. I've never believed that you have to take the devil's money to pay the Lord's bills."

Though she avoided appearances in secular settings that could perhaps have resulted in greater earthly rewards, Francine Morrison made her mark in this world. She recorded several best-selling albums. She played piano and sang for Dr. Martin Luther King when he visited Fort Worth in 1959. She was thrilled to perform once with Mahalia Jackson, a singer to whom she was often compared. She toured the world, singing and praying.

"Hers was a soulful, deep-rooted gospel voice that could touch the heart and sting the soul," said Fort Worth journalist Bob Ray Sanders when Morrison died in 2016. "Depending on the song she was singing, it was like hearing the very sound of the angel Gabriel's trumpet—every part of your being felt every piercing note."

Throughout North Texas—a shiny buckle in the western stretches of the Bible Belt—gospel artists have long produced such heightened experiences among their listeners. An especially memorable example took place on New Year's Eve, 1925, when Fort Worth's WBAP broadcast the "singing, shouting, and preaching" of "an old-time negro revival" at the Trezevent Road Church of God in Christ.

"Specially arranged microphones will allow no part of the service to escape the unseen audience," promised the *Fort Worth Star-Telegram*, casting the "program of unusual interest" in an anthropological context as "one of the greatest novelties ever offered the radio public." The WBAP announcer, the Hired Hand, was on duty for play-by-play narration. A young blind woman named Arizona Dranes supplied music for the service.

One who tuned in that night was George R. Bradford of the Consolidated Talking Machine Company of Chicago, owners of the OKeh record label. As the *Star-Telegram* reported the following September, in an article headlined "BLIND NEGRO PIANO PLAYER OF FORT WORTH WINS NOTICE WITH PHONOGRAPH RECORDS," the "peculiar quality" of Arizona Dranes's spirited vocals and barrelhouse keyboards caught Bradford's ear and resulted in a recording contract. Her "blending of religious airs with syncopation" produced a "startling" effect.

Or as gospel researcher Michael Corcoran put it nearly a century later, "Dranes and her lost-in-the-spirit outbursts laid the blueprint for rock 'n' roll."

For a time in the midtwenties, Arizona Dranes appears to have lived in both Fort Worth and in the State Thomas neighborhood of Dallas, not far from Deep Ellum, where she likely heard pounding piano blues floating down the sidewalk with a ghostly moan. Contrary to some accounts, however, none of her recording sessions took place in Dallas, according to Corcoran's research. But the city did produce remarkable recordings by Washington Phillips, playing his unique "manzarene," a one-of-a-kind, double-zither instrument, and by Blind Willie Johnson, with his otherworldly vocals and groundbreaking slide guitar.

While Anglo-American gospel music may have generally seemed more staid and conventional than the sounds produced by their African American brethren, their musical missions were also fueled by fire, brimstone, and amazing grace. The Stamps-Baxter Music Company, which moved its headquarters to Dallas from Jacksonville, Texas, in 1929, touched millions with their songbooks and hymnals, radio broadcasts, and live performances by some thirty-four Stamps-Baxter quartets that toured nationwide.

Dallas radio station KRLD wanted the Stamps-Baxter singers to restrict their on-air program to patriotic and pop songs when they performed in a glass booth at the Texas Centennial in 1936, according to a story told the *Oak Cliff Advocate* by David Spence, who recently renovated the gospel company's former North Tyler Street building. Instead, the group launched into a religious number and told listeners to send the station a telegram if they liked the music. Thousands of telegrams received, KRLD boosted its religious programming and its signal, from 10,000 to 50,000 watts. Stamps-Baxter programming also boomed out from Dr. John R. Brinkley's super-powered border-blaster XERA, down along the silvery Rio Grande.

Stamps-Baxter's singing school and singing conventions spawned the popular "all-night sings" in Dallas. Starting in the late 1930s, the annual gatherings appear to have lasted into the early 1960s, moving from the Cotton Bowl to the Sportatorium (home of the *Big "D" Jamboree*) and other locations. Thousands showed up to "stay all night, stay a little longer" and enjoy the uplifting sounds from dozens of gospel quartets.

While Stamps-Baxter singers were going religiously rogue on KRLD during the Centennial in Dallas, over in Fort Worth the Chuck Wagon Gang was beginning a long gospel reign on WBAP. The family group began in Lubbock in 1935 when Dave Carter arranged for an audition at local radio station KYFO. Aiming simply to spread the word and to enjoy the pleasures of making music, Dave also hoped to earn a little money to buy medicine for his ailing wife, Carrie.

The original Lubbock Carter Family lineup included Dave, tenor and mandolin; son Ernest, bass voice and guitar; daughter Rosa Lola, soprano; and daughter Effie, alto. After moving to Fort Worth and the increased wattage of WBAP in 1936, big-city media strategists changed their

Blind Willie Johnson lived and recorded in Dallas in the late 1920s. In 1977, his singular performances on record were among the sounds of earth launched into space aboard the Voyager spacecraft, where they remain ready to introduce non-earthlings to our music. Courtesy of Marshall Wyatt, Old Hat Records.

Courtesy of George Gimarc.

"Good Morning, Friends!"

"TEXAS' FAVORITE QUARTETS"

Heard daily from KRLD

THE STAMPS QUARTET

THE JUNIOR QUARTET

$10.00 for a Name for our new songbook that we are publishing for schools. If you like to sing you will want one of the books. If you order the book now, in advance of publication, you may suggest a name for the book; if the name you send is the one selected you will receive a nice, new, crisp $10.00 bill. Tell all your friends about this contest; any of them may enter if they are of school age. An order for one of the books must accompany each name suggested. The book will come to you just as soon as it comes from the press. We pay the postage, and the price is only 25 cents. A description of the book will be found on the back of this folder. Show it to your friends.

After the Stamps-Baxter Co. moved to Dallas in 1929, it reached hundreds of thousands, if not millions, with its songbooks, thirty-four touring quartets, singing schools, radio broadcasts, and "all-night sings." Courtesy of George Gimarc.

Courtesy of George Gimarc.

Jewell Blanton Kelly, award-winning choir director and music educator, grew up attending Rising Star Baptist Church in Fort Worth. A graduate of North Texas State, she taught in FWISD for fifty years. Her students included Kirk Franklin, who got his start as choir director at Stranger's Rest Baptist Church in Como. The Black Musicians Association of Tarrant County celebrated her achievements as a "Living Legend Honoree" in 2019. Courtesy of Jewell Blanton Kelly.

names to Dad, Jim, Rose, and Anna. Sponsored by Bewley Mills, the group's name was changed to the Chuck Wagon Gang, not to be confused with several earlier (and at least one contemporaneous) iterations of the Chuck Wagon Gang. Also popular on WBAP, the previous Chuck Wagon Gangs did include hymns in their varied repertoire. Two of the new Gang's most enduring songs appeared on their early recordings, "A Beautiful Life" and "I'd Rather Have Jesus."

As music historian Joe Specht notes in *The Handbook of Texas Music*, Dad Carter grew up singing in the shape-note tradition, and much of the Chuck Wagon Gang's material was drawn from the shape-note songbooks published by Stamps-Baxter. The group was also the first to record Albert Brumley's classic, "I'll Fly Away."

The Gang headed east after leaving WBAP in 1950, and, dozens of quartet members later, still performs under the name today. In 2019 the Chuck Wagon Gang released the album *No Depression in Heaven: The Gospel Songs of the Carter Family*, consisting of material recorded by the other Carter Family that featured A. P., Sara, Helen, June, Anita, and Mother Maybelle.

Another Fort Worth gospel group still active into this century, the Singing Wills Family, also shares a surname with a landmark secular ensemble. A. B. "Pop" Wills grew up picking cotton in Hall County alongside his first cousin, Texas Playboys bandleader Bob Wills. Pop started the Wills Family Quartet in Hall County in 1938 with his three oldest children. They performed at Stamps-Baxter singing conventions, and most, if not all seven, of the Wills children, including youngest son Bob L. Wills, attended Stamps-Baxter Music School in the summertime.

In 1982, one of the kids, Calvin Wills, recalled with a sense of humor that the art of making a joyful noise unto the Lord also required hard work and discipline. "We learned our do-re-mi's before the A-B-C's," he said. "That was a must. Dad always used to say that if the little ones didn't try to sing, he was going to take them out and drown them. But we weren't worried. There wasn't much water in that dust bowl around Amarillo."

When Calvin Wills died in 2003, a memorial benefit concert at Johnnie High's Arlington Music Hall raised funds for a future Gospel Museum of Texas. For years the museum, a collection of gospel concert posters, hymnals and songbooks, vintage records, early recording equipment, and rare photos had occupied a bus that Calvin drove in parades and parked at performances. Today the museum continues on the Internet, its brick-and-mortar presence still a gospel community dream.

When the museum is built someday, its hall of fame will certainly reserve a place of honor for another Fort Worth gospel star, Kirk Franklin. Raised by a great-great-great-aunt who collected cans to pay for his music lessons, Franklin was singing at Mount Zion Baptist Church by the age of six. At age seventeen (or perhaps even younger) he was the music minister at Greater Stranger's Rest Missionary Baptist Church in the Como neighborhood.

Kirk Franklin brought a new style to the congregation's services. Stranger's Rest Pastor R. E. West later told *Ebony* magazine, "I brought in the drums, the microphone and then here comes this little kid who gets up and dances and bounces. The older people couldn't stand it. But eventually, he won them over."

The Carter family gospel group came to Fort Worth in 1936. They were soon broadcasting on WBAP as the Chuck Wagon Gang, remaining on the Fort Worth station until 1950. Courtesy of Ted Tucker.

Courtesy of George Gimarc.

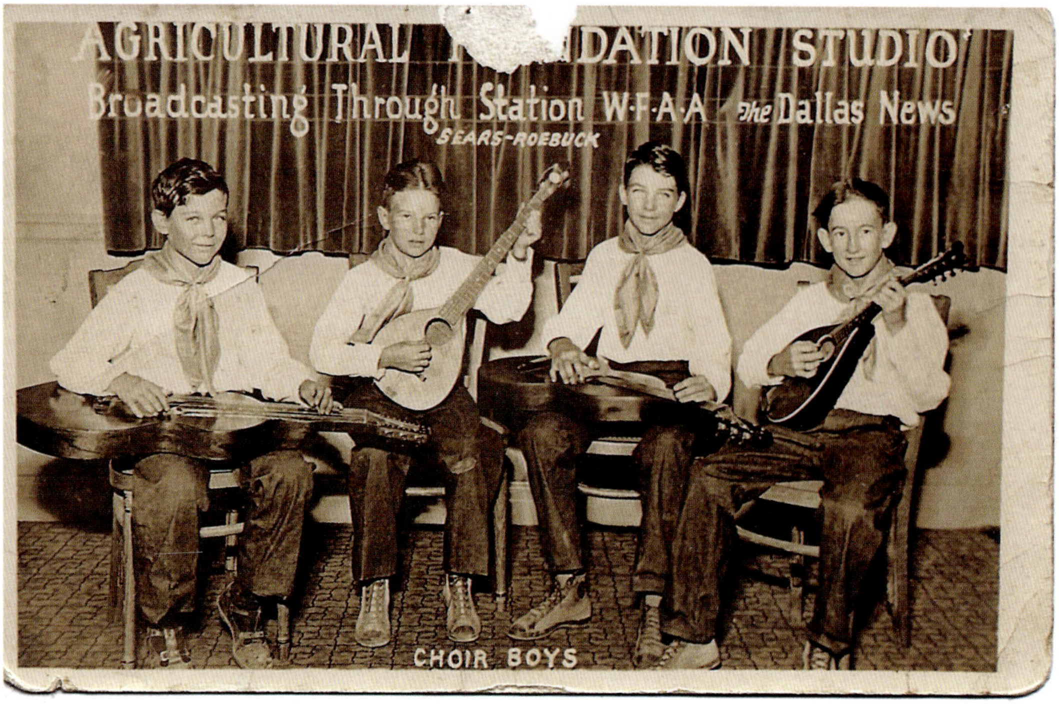

These sharp-looking Choir Boys performed at the Texas State Fair's Agricultural Foundation Studio in, as best we can determine, 1925. Courtesy of Terry Williams.

Six-year-old Lorraine Miles leads Sacred Harp singers in a rendition of "The Last Words of Copernicus" at a singing convention in Mineral Wells, circa 1930. Courtesy of Chloe Webb.

Violinist Dorothy Tilson, third from right in the front row, told her daughter Patti that Mr. Pulliam always had a pet monkey with him. Beyond that, his Sacred Orchestra remains something of a mystery. Courtesy of Patti Tilson.

Several of the five musical Jessup brothers had a ministerial presence in the metroplex. Darrell Jessup is shown here at 1939 tent revival in Fort Worth. Courtesy of Donna Donnell.

Evangelist J. Charles Jessup's Fellowship Revival Association was based in Fort Worth, though he also maintained a base in Gulfport, Mississippi. Shown here during a Fort Worth revival in 1939, Jessup's radio ministry reached a wide audience over the powerful border radio stations located in Mexico. His ministry ran afoul of federal authorities, and Brother Jessup spent time in prison. Courtesy of Donna Donnell.

Rapturea Records was run by Rev. Emmett J. Lee of the Eminent Twilight Singers. He also ran the Hosanna label in the 1970s. Rev. Lee still pastors today at the Rapturea Better Way Ministry in Dallas. Many North Texas gospel groups recorded on these labels, including the Relatives and the Fort Worth Spiritual Airs. Courtesy of George Gimarc.

When he became musical director of the DFW Mass Choir, gospel radio personality Drew Dawson marveled, "Kirk Franklin is probably the most talented individual I've ever met. He plays a choir like it's a piano." In 1993, Franklin's first album, *Kirk Franklin and The Family*, sold more copies than any debut gospel record in history.

Mixing hip-hop, R & B, and funk with gospel, his successive recordings—*Whatcha Lookin' 4*, *God's Property from Kirk Franklin's Nu Nation*, *The Rebirth of Kirk Franklin*, *Long Live Love*, and others—continued winning Grammy awards and selling in the millions. "What sets Franklin apart from the pack as a writer," noted Dave Ferman in the *Star-Telegram* in 2002, "is his ability to pen both quiet, piano-based ballads and hard-hitting, funk-based tracks, while giving his songs a this-is-my-life-right-now immediacy so often lacking in gospel composers."

Still, there were detractors. When *Vibe* magazine ran a profile on Franklin, one reader, sounding like he or she had never seen fundamentalists get down, wrote, "It's hard to believe that *Stomp* is a church song. The people in the video gyrate, throw their hair wildly, shake their bodies, and Kirk even does the Snake."

Unfazed, "Kid Fresh" Franklin from the streets of Cowtown told one interviewer, "God can fit into our culture. God can be cool."

Of course, even highly original artists stand on the shoulders of giants. Osmotic influences on

Franklin's music must surely include the Relatives, founded in Dallas in 1970 by pastors Gean West and Tommie West. The brothers had grown up in a family described in publicity as "Dallas gospel royalty." In the 1950s and '60s, when it was still difficult for black touring artists to find hotels, the West home hosted such performers as a young Aretha Franklin, the Mighty Clouds of Joy, and the Staples Singers.

The West brothers' music was "spawned from the same fervent Pentecostal tradition that begat Elder Utah Smith," but the Relatives' raw funkadelic sound often confused otherwise spirited congregations. Still, the group managed to tour through the disco decade, releasing a handful of 45 rpm records that fell into obscurity after the Relatives broke up in 1980 and the West brothers settled into rewarding pastorships of small Dallas churches.

Then sometime in the 1990s, Billie Buck scored a copy of a Relatives 45, "Don't Let Me Fall," at a Fort Worth thrift store or garage sale and passed it along to her son, the blue-chip blues drummer, Mike Buck. When he shared the scratchy treasure with Noel Waggener of Heavy Light Records, the archival producer began a years-long quest to find the Relatives and reissue the song. Stellar Dallas engineer Phil York still had masters for other Relatives' seventies tracks, and that led to the group's first album, 2009's *Don't Let Me Fall*.

A career resurgence followed, with performances at Austin City Limits, Bonnaroo, Lincoln Center, etc. Before Rev. Gean West's death in 2015, a second album, *The Electric Word*, was issued on the Yep Roc label. Though the Relatives were surely never part of the drug culture, accolades from a wide range of admirers included this metaphorical stunner from Leo Sacks. "The Relatives," wrote the Grammy-winning producer, "are Jesus on LSD."

As detailed in one of his album's liner notes, Richard Miller was born in Dallas County in 1942 "without hands and feet. Yet he plays the organ and guitar." Responding to the desire to make music as a child, Richard made some country-western records that were issued on his own Garland-based label, Richard Miller Record Co. One disc featured two Hank Thompson compositions, "Greenlight" and "Don't Flirt With Me." In 1964, he released a single on the assassination of President Kennedy. After a successful gospel career, Miller retired to Nogales, Mexico, where he was found murdered in 2017. Courtesy of George Gimarc.

Unknown gospel artists, deep in the spirit, Fort Worth. Courtesy of Donna Donnell.

Gean West and the Relatives! Courtesy of Matt Wright-Steel.

The extended Williams Family would "party and make a joyful noise on Saturday nights, and give thanks and praise on Sunday mornings." As the sons and daughters of the family put it, "We always had such a good time together, we didn't even know we were dirt-poor." In this photo, Aline Williams, married to Gilford "Bud" Williams of the Williams Boys from Paris, Texas, is providing accompaniment to a gospel hymn. Courtesy of William Williams.

Traveling evangelists P. F. Morgan and Mrs. Morgan traveled in a customized Ford that included a kitchenette, a small reception room, and a foldaway bed. Both Morgans sang and preached, accompanied by P. F. on a harp guitar. Courtesy of John Slate.

Cheri Robbins belts out a tune in a setting that normally hosted metroplex livestock auctions. Courtesy of George Gimarc

CHAPTER SIX

Music at Large

Hath Charms to Soothe

Music, of course, wafts through the world in countless contexts beyond the concert hall, nightclub, and broadcasting station. Music likes to bust out of its regular confines and serve humankind with its therapeutic mojo in a great multiplicity of settings and contexts . . . at times, whether we like it or not.

Music, the saying goes, hath charms to soothe the savage beast. The famous phrase is actually an escapee from the 1697 play *The Mourning Bride*, by the poet William Congreve, who wrote, "Musick has Charms to sooth a savage Breast, / To soften Rocks, or bend a knotted Oak. / I've read, that things inanimate have mov'd, / And, as with living Souls, have been inform'd, / By Magick Numbers and persuasive Sound, / What then am I? Am I more senseless grown / Than Trees, or Flint? O force of constant Woe! / 'Til not in Harmony to calm my Griefs." Over time the quote has evolved from "breast" to "beast."

But we digress. Whatever Congreve's problem was, there's no denying that music is powerful stuff. The Boneheads of Dallas certainly knew that. While the members of this venerable brotherhood—founded in 1919 on principles of everyday civic surrealism—may not have been trained musicians, they were not reluctant to take up instruments and sally forth with a sonic assault when the situation demanded . . . or they simply got the urge. One such experimental music episode occurred in December 1951.

In a *Dallas Morning News* story headlined "Boneheads Lose in Noise Contest," Frank X. Tolbert wrote, "The Bonehead Club suffered one of its rare defeats in the premeditated humor department Friday." Columnist Tolbert went on to explain that the club's fifty-seven vice presidents (the Boneheads had fifty-seven vice presidents because of the urban advertising legend that Heinz had fifty-seven varieties of ketchup—there was no Bonehead president) marched in to disrupt the weekly luncheon of the Dallas Advertising League, but was out-pranked by the Fifties Mad Men, who had a Salvation Army Band standing by to drown out the Boneheads.

At the following week's luncheon, the Boneheads unexpectedly returned, crashing the affair with "roof-raising drumming and ear-shattering tromboning," followed by a string trio that sawed awfully away on "Five Foot Two." The ad league president, reported an unsigned *News* piece, "ordered his sergeant-at-arms to oust the intruders, but was betrayed by his own colleagues. Some of them pitched pennies at the musicians." Bonehead musical performances depicted in the images included here may or may not represent these particular commando concerts.

The following gallery captures North Texans making and enjoying music in a variety of sometimes unexpected settings.

Some of the fifty-seven vice presidents of the Boneheads, a Dallas club founded "for no particular reason," play musical instruments....or, perhaps more accurately, produce sound that would have warmed the hearts of John Cage and Groucho Marx. Courtesy of Dallas Public Library.

This image may represent the Bonehead string trio that slaughtered the popular tune "Five Foot Two" after crashing the Dallas Ad League luncheon in December 1951. Courtesy of Dallas Public Library.

Margaret Wilson, on accordion, and guitarist Duenne Collins endure the spirited hijinx of tipsy lawyers at Eagle Mountain Lake during the 1940s Texas Bar Association Convention held in Fort Worth. Courtesy of *Fort Worth Star-Telegram* Collection, University of Texas at Arlington Special Collections.

The Future Farmer Band of Corsicana provided music for a 1940 Navarro County farm club picnic. Left to right: Dawson Thedford, Jimmy Morris, Claud Willis, Skee Williams, R. L. Barron (adviser for the Corsicana Future Farmers of America), and Jack Hoffman. Courtesy of *Fort Worth Star-Telegram* Collection, University of Texas at Arlington Special Collections.

Robert Rohleder, known as the Bing Crosby of Western Union, sings a birthday telegram to Fort Worth on the city's ninety-first anniversary in 1940. Courtesy of *Fort Worth Star-Telegram* Collection, University of Texas at Arlington Special Collections.

"There's nothing like a song to chase the blues away." These North Texas servicemen may have suspected in 1940 that the United States would inevitably be drawn into the conflict raging overseas. But whatever troubles they may have had were suspended for the moment by the joy of singing. Left to right: J. L. Aaron, cook, Sergeant J. B. Aaron, Private E. C. Manning, Sergeant G. D. Winnegar, and Corporal Spud Summers. Courtesy of *Fort Worth Star-Telegram* Collection, University of Texas at Arlington Special Collections.

Band serenades bronc riders, steer wrestlers

Before his death in 1989 at age sixty-one, Lew Gillis—music teacher, writer, singer, trombonist, and sound engineer—had participated as musician and conductor with the Fort Worth Stock Show Rodeo Band for forty-four years. He was a mentor, friend, and inspiration to a myriad of great DFW musicians, providing many with good union employment in what was considered to be "the best Rodeo Band in the country." Courtesy of Nancy Gillis.

Back in the day, says *Hometown by Handlebar* blogger Mike Nichols, just about every Fort Worth institution with a pulse had its own band. The city sported its own band, as did the police department and each local packing plant. The Shriners, Masons, local railroad outposts, bottling plants, department stores, candy companies, furniture companies, parks, automobile dealers...they all had bands. Several churches maintained orchestras. In Weatherford, the Knights of Pythias home had an all-female mandolin orchestra with thirty-three members. Shown here is the Montgomery Ward Trail Blazers Band, with band director and police officer Frank Maco holding the baton. Courtesy of Mike Nichols, hometownbyhandlebar.com.

Like many sixties bands, Fort Worth's Barons, with Johnny Nitzinger, often played promotional gigs. Here the boys do their thing on a flatbed truck rolling through downtown Fort Worth behind local car dealer Bill "Batman" McDavid's Batmobile. Courtesy of Larry Harrison.

The elaborate Texas Spring Palace, part agricultural fair and part educational, cultural, and entertainment center, opened in May 1889 but burned to the ground during its second season in May 1890. Nonetheless, many North Texans and other visitors enjoyed performances in the structure by the Elgin Watch Factory Band, the Mexican National Band, and other music groups, including the unnamed orchestra pictured here. Courtesy of Tarrant County Archives.

The Spring Palace even had its own specially composed music. Courtesy of University of Texas at Arlington Special Collections.

"Tell your friends/You'll meet them in Dallas,/In the town/Where there is no malice." So went the tune composed by Jack Gardner, orchestra leader and entertainment manager at Dallas's Adolphus Hotel. "Approved" by the mayor, the song was created to persuade the Democratic Party to hold its 1916 national convention in Dallas. Democrats convened in St. Louis that year instead. Courtesy of University of Texas at Arlington Special Collections.

Hugh Fowler shakes hands with Barry Goldwater at a Dallas rally for the senator's campaign for president in 1964. Hugh Fowler Orchestra musicians can be seen in the lower right corner. Courtesy of Trinity River Music.

I. M. Terrell graduate and drummer Ronald Shannon Jackson founded his own band, the Decoding Society, in 1979, mixing experimental jazz with rock and funk. Jackson's father operated the city's only black-owned record store, and his mother played piano and organ for the Methodist church. "He was a very forward-looking and free-thinking musician. He was always questioning things," said Ken Shimamoto, a local writer and musician, when Jackson died in 2013. "He had an inquisitive mind and a restless intelligence that manifested itself in everything he did musically." Courtesy of Ronald Shannon Jackson.

CHAPTER SEVEN

Jazz, Big Bands

That Different Music

Dallas native Leroy "Hog" Cooper, who played sax with Ray Charles for twenty years, reminisced about the music scene at the Jim Hotel in Fort Worth. "I also remember . . . when this funny-looking kid with long hair was walkin' around in the hallways with his saxophone, playin' that different music to himself. That was Ornette Coleman."

In time, the saxophonist Cooper found "funny-looking" grew to be quite dapper and distinguished, but his music—driven by an esoteric theory Coleman called "harmolodics"—evolved to become so unique that jazz fans and musicians alike either grooved to its grammar of sound or fled the performance hall in confusion and even disgust. Whichever, the 1948 graduate of Fort Worth's I. M. Terrell High School was recognized with the 2007 Pulitzer Prize for Music.

Coleman first saw a saxophone when Sonny Strain and his Sultans of Swing came to play for his classmates at George Washington Carver Elementary School. Entranced, he shined shoes and saved up for years to buy his first instrument. Before long, he was playing with a fifty-piece group at Greater St. James Baptist Church. At I. M. Terrell, where the band was led by the jazz-shunning instructor G. A. Baxter, Ornette was often in hot water for improvising during performances of John Philip Sousa marches.

As Chris Vaughn reported in the *Fort Worth Star-Telegram* in 2003, Coleman, like many other young Fort Worth musicians, "grew up fast in the nightclubs along Rosedale Street and Evans Avenue—the Zanzibar, nationally known for its retractable roof; the China Doll; the Paradise Inn; the Zebra Lounge." One of his first professional gigs was with a band led by local tenor saxophonist Red Connor. When he finally got to play a solo, during the classic *Star Dust*, Coleman could not resist improvising and was soon unemployed as a result. After an early-career performance in Baton Rouge, he was beaten by some club patrons offended by his unique style and the "Jesus-like beard" he wore at the time.

While Ornette may have been unique and the best-known jazzman to emerge from Fort Worth, the city produced a surprising number of important jazz musicians. Of all Texas's major cities, notes Dave Oliphant in his 1996 book, *Texan Jazz*, "it might seem highly unlikely that Cowtown, as Fort Worth has been called since its early days as a center for cattle auctions, slaughterhouses, packing plants, and a railhead for shipping, would give rise to the most avant-garde movement in jazz since bebop."

They include such artists as saxophonists, clarinet players, and flautists Dewey Redman, Red Connor, Julius Hemphill, John Carter, King Curtis Ousley, Prince Lasha, Ben Martin, and Fronzelle Littlefield; trumpet player Jeep Smith; and percussionists Charles Moffett and Ronald Shannon Jackson. "Dallas was much bigger than Fort Worth," Jackson told *Musician, Player, and Listener* in 1981, "but Fort Worth always had the cats who were on the money in terms of the music."

Most of these musicians matriculated from I. M. Terrell. And many, as noted, played sax. "Fort Worth has produced more avant-garde saxophonists than any city in the world except

Chicago," Fort Worth blues guitarist Sumter Bruton III said in 1994. "Why that is I can't really explain."

While I. M. Terrell High School produced important musicians in Fort Worth, Lincoln High School in Dallas, which opened in 1939, eventually graduated such artists as saxophonists David "Fathead" Newman, Buster Smith, and Leroy Cooper; pianist and saxophonist Fran Gaddison; flautist and vocalist Bobbi Humphrey; singers Marilyn Walton and Shirley McFatter; pianist Cedar Walton; and trumpeter Bobby Bradford. Other Dallas schools produced saxophonist and clarinetist Budd Johnson, sax players John Hardee and John Handy, saxophonist/flautist James Clay, trombonists Dan Minor and Keg Johnson, and trumpet players Claude "Benno" Kennedy and Oran "Hot Lips" Page.

Red Garland began playing alto sax at Booker T. Washington High School in Dallas and took up piano while serving in the army during World War II. Like most of these musicians, Garland had to leave the Dallas-Fort Worth area to find opportunities to play the exploratory style of music he preferred. After the war he joined bands led by fellow Dallasites Henry "Buster" Smith and Oran "Hot Lips" Page; in the late '40s, Red "bebopped" alongside Charlie Parker. Early in the 1950s, he collaborated with John Coltrane, and later that decade he was a member of the Miles Davis Quintet.

Courtesy of George Gimarc.

Fort Worth's "Fabulous, Dazzling Zanzibar" at 951 East Rosedale was owned by the "glamorous Creole" Lucylle Horne, seen on the left in the photo above at Zanzibar's opening with bandleader Bertrand Adams and former Dallasite Dorothy Delaney.

Harmolodics creator Ornette Coleman returns home to Fort Worth with his band Prime Time for a performance at the grand opening of Caravan of Dreams in 1983. Courtesy of University of Texas at Arlington Special Collections.

Ronald Shannon Jackson.
Courtesy of Ronald Shannon Jackson.

Left to right: Denardo Coleman, Ornette Coleman, Ed Bass, Texas Music Office director Casey Monahan, at the Governor's Mansion, circa 2007, on the occasion of Ornette receiving the Texas Arts Medal. Courtesy of Casey Monahan.

Born in Corsicana in 1933, saxophonist/flautist David "Fathead" Newman moved to Dallas with his family at age two. Over the course of a long career, he played with Ray Charles, Buster Smith, T-Bone Walker, Aretha Franklin, B. B. King, Dr. John, and many others. Back in Dallas for a time in the 1960s, he led the horn section of *The !!!! Beat,* a soul and R & B show on Dallas TV. Explaining his unique nickname, he said, "I was in band class and I had this music on my music stand but it was upside down.... He [J. K. Miller, his band teacher] knew I could barely read the music right side up. He thumped me on the head and called me 'Fathead.' My classmates laughed. After that, it became my trademark. I don't consider it derogatory and it doesn't offend me." He added, though, that he preferred David. Newman's final recording, *The Blessing,* appeared in 2009, the same year he died. Courtesy of Carl Sidle.

Saxophonist Rachella Parks-Washington's music blends gospel, jazz, and pop. A graduate of the University of North Texas, the Fort Worth-based artist has played at festivals throughout the US and Europe. Her CD, *Meditative Inspirational Suite,* was inspired by her struggles with the disease sarcoidosis. Courtesy of Fort Worth Public Library.

Garland returned to live in Dallas for the last nineteen years of his life, playing regularly in his hometown. Fort Worth musician and writer Ken Shimamoto reported that Ronald Shannon Jackson also returned home in 1996, spending "the rest of his life in his family's house on North Judkins Street near Riverside Drive [in Fort Worth], surrounded by artwork, books and records, instruments and memorabilia of his career. . . . Saxophonist Rachella Parks-Washington played in some of his last bands, and local musicians Curtis Heath and Britt Robisheaux worked with Shannon on archiving his library of unreleased recordings." Jackson played his last gig at Dallas's Kessler Theater in 2012 before his death the following year.

Dewey Redman returned home in 2003 to play the Jazz by the Boulevard Festival. Fort Worth's beloved jazz enthusiast Marjorie Crenshaw told Redman about the Big D 60s internet group that had recently been launched to document metroplex rock 'n' roll history, and shortly thereafter, Redman reached out to its founders to express his wish that Dallas-Fort Worth's jazz legacy might be similarly preserved.

When *Star-Telegram* writer Christopher Evans interviewed Redman in late 1993, the musician reminisced about discovering "a whole new world" of sound on "the rambunctious corner of East Rosedale Avenue and Evans Avenue" on the city's southeast side. "Fort Worth," said Redman, "that's my theme. I'm just a country boy from Fort Worth, who came to New York and made it."

In New York, Redman was for a time "the other saxophonist" in Ornette Coleman's quartet. And the group's leader offered praise. "Dewey," said Coleman, "is the freshest and deepest natural player I played with in quite some years."

Dave Oliphant noted some of the saxophonists' similarities. "Dewey does not stick to any one style, even though he, like Ornette, retains always a touch of the blues feeling from his early days in R & B groups in Texas."

While metroplex high schools were graduating fine jazz musicians, the music program at University of North Texas in Denton began offering the world's first university degrees in jazz studies in the late 1940s. Stan Kenton recruited musicians from the program for his band. UNT produced such renowned artists as jazz cellist Harry Babasinian, pianist Gene Roland, and multi-instrumentalist Jimmy Giuffre. Guitarist Herb Ellis, a native of Farmersville near Dallas, studied string

Born on a North Texas cotton farm in 1904, saxophonist Henry "Buster" Smith, who later became a mentor to Charlie Parker, bought his first instrument, a clarinet, with money made picking cotton. The family soon moved into Dallas, where Buster was exposed to a new world of music. "Man, Deep Ellum was wide open," Smith said in a 1987 Tim Schuller piece. People would "hang out by the railroad tracks and listen at the medicine shows, and then go to the Tip Top." Though he traveled widely with the Blue Devils and other name bands after leaving Dallas, this image of his own band at the Cocoanut Grove, identified in Dallas Public Library notes as circa 1946, was most likely taken at the club by that name in Dallas because the photographer was Marion Butts. And it is also believed that Smith ceased touring in 1941 and returned to Dallas. Courtesy of Ted Tucker.

Courtesy of Dallas Public Library.

Jan.-April 1999 The Dallas/Fort Worth Musician 5

YESTERYEAR

Local 72-147 Executive Board Member and Convention Delegate ***Marjorie Crenshaw****, is shown at left above in this 1952 photo with* ***Duke Ellington****. Her friend, Mary Frances Clemmons, appears above right. Ms. Crenshaw visited with Ellington during intermission at an engagement at the Blue Note in Chicago that year.*

LIFE LINES

Marjorie Crenshaw, Fort Worth's beloved jazz historian and mentor, died in 2019 at age ninety-one. She met many important artists who came to Fort Worth, including Duke Ellington, seen here with Crenshaw, but she valued the musical experiences of her students just as much as the greats. She began playing piano and organ in church and discovered jazz on a trip to New Orleans with her mother. "I never thought of myself as a jazz musician because I wanted to see the notes," she told the DFW Musicians Union in 2018, "but then someone in church came up and told me that what I was playing was jazz. I just learned how to feel it." Courtesy of Fort Worth Public Library.

Courtesy of Fort Worth Public Library.

bass during his UNT days but went on to grace the Oscar Peterson Trio and many other ensembles with his six-string virtuosity. As Les Paul said of Ellis, "If you're not swinging, he's gonna make you swing."

While most progressive jazz musicians from Dallas and Fort Worth left the area to pursue their artistic visions, Cowtown pianist Johnny Case stuck to his guns and did it his way in his hometown. Born in 1947, Johnny and his older brother Jerry, a guitarist, grew up in a musical family. Dad J. C. Case played mandolin and sang harmony with Bill Case and his Melody Boys, and mother Floy Case was a trailblazing country-western journalist. Johnny and Jerry were child performers on the *Red River Jamboree* and other country and western programs and venues. But by age fifteen, Johnny says, the young musician knew that jazz was his "true calling."

The teenage pianist continued working with country-dance ensembles as he made the gradual transition to jazz. He played with Ray Chaney and his Ranch Hands at Chaney's Stagecoach Ballroom (located at the time in the old Crystal Springs Ballroom), and in early 1966 vocalist Joe Andrews (a Texas Playboys alum) hired Johnny for the new house band at Dallas's Aragon Ballroom. "This ten-piece ensemble was the finest

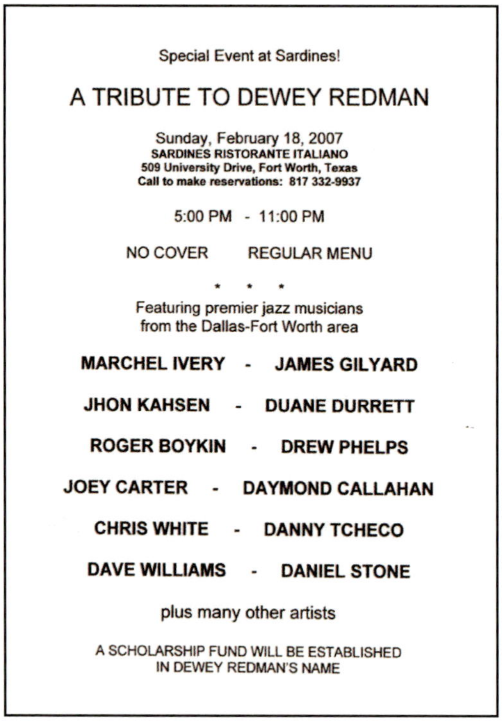

Special Event at Sardines!

A TRIBUTE TO DEWEY REDMAN

Sunday, February 18, 2007
SARDINES RISTORANTE ITALIANO
509 University Drive, Fort Worth, Texas
Call to make reservations: 817 332-9937

5:00 PM - 11:00 PM

NO COVER REGULAR MENU

* * *

Featuring premier jazz musicians
from the Dallas-Fort Worth area

MARCHEL IVERY - JAMES GILYARD
JHON KAHSEN - DUANE DURRETT
ROGER BOYKIN - DREW PHELPS
JOEY CARTER - DAYMOND CALLAHAN
CHRIS WHITE - DANNY TCHECO
DAVE WILLIAMS - DANIEL STONE

plus many other artists

A SCHOLARSHIP FUND WILL BE ESTABLISHED
IN DEWEY REDMAN'S NAME

The Fort Worth jazz community paid tribute to Dewey Redman. Courtesy of Johnny Case.

Jazz pianist Johnny Case has forged a long career at home in Fort Worth on his own artistic terms. Johnny and his guitarist brother Jerry began as child performers with country-western and western swing bands. In 1983, Johnny began a twenty-eight-year performing run at Sardines Ristorante Italiano, which could be a record for the longest-running nightly jazz gig. Courtesy of Johnny Case.

Fort Worth native Quamon Fowler is accomplished on both the saxophone and the electronic wind instrument. Fowler has produced seven CDs, and he has served as artist-in-residence at Southwestern Seminary's School of Church Music in Fort Worth. His latest recording is entitled *With You*. Courtesy of Carl Sidle.

western swing band I had played with," says Case, "and I only left the Aragon in late summer to realize the beginning of my dream."

Late that same year, 1966, Case met jazz pianist Thomas Reese, an established artist on the metroplex scene. "I'd heard him perform with the Julius Hemphill Quartet, which participated as the intermission band at a concert by the Ornette Coleman Trio. This was my first hearing of alto saxophonist Hemphill, who led his group through a set of standards, played with fire and creative spirit equal to that of the headliner's more adventurous free jazz. Hemphill's bassist Louie Spears was familiar from having heard him with the Red Garland Trio performing at the Arandis in Dallas. . . . I would soon leave western swing to pursue my dream of playing jazz, so the opportunity to hear this group was an unexpected treat, added to this unusual Fort Worth booking of Ornette by his sister Trudy Coleman. In hearing the pianist Reese, two things relating to my own musical development were immediately clear: First, I realized immediately that I still had much work, or 'woodshedding' to do. Second, I felt that attaining the degree of artistic proficiency I heard in the playing of Thomas Reese was within my grasp, given that I was quite determined to find my way into this exciting genre of music."

Johnny Case's first jazz gig was with the Adrian Watts Trio at the historic Texas Hotel in downtown Fort Worth. As the years rolled along, he supplemented the relatively infrequent opportunities for jazz by picking up recording and live performance work in pop, c&w, western swing, and "society" bands. He recorded his first jazz LP in 1969 "under a spell of mystical creativity. . . . I loved the avant-garde and the ideal of a totally improvised music that could sustain interest and prove to be of lasting value."

The pianist landed a six-nights-a-week job at J. R.'s Place in Fort Worth in 1980, and in September 1983, he began a twenty-eight-year run at Sardines Ristorante Italiano. "I probably hold the record for the longest-running nightly jazz gig," he muses, "playing solo piano weeknights and trio on weekends." In nearly three decades of performances, the Fort Worth jazz musician seldom missed a performance. He took off one evening to play a reception for Ornette Coleman at the opening of Fort Worth's legendary jazz club, Caravan of Dreams.

James Clay, "the Kid from Dallas," played tenor sax with Ray Charles, Ornette Coleman, David "Fathead" Newman, Don Cherry, and many others. But he didn't care for the limelight, often moving back to Dallas to take a break from higher-profile musical activity. Bassist Red Mitchell said in a 1957 interview, "As for James Clay, I think he could end up laying the foundation for maybe the next step in jazz. He's already mastered at an early age the things that the rest of us seem to be wallowing around trying to get." Bassist Drew Phelps, who played with Clay at Dallas's Recovery Room from 1981 to 1983, said, "He was mysterious, an eccentric kind of guy, but a great player with a charismatic sound." Courtesy of Sumter Bruton.

Trumpeter and flugelhornist Roy Hargrove began playing at age nine when he found a cornet his factory worker father had bought at a Dallas pawnshop. As a student at Booker T. Washington High School, he met the visiting Wynton Marsalis, who became a mentor. In a career cut short by cardiac arrest at age forty-nine in 2018, Hargrove's varied output included such albums as 2009's *Emergence,* which the *Guardian* described as "a sophisticated confection of Ray Charlesian bluesiness, hip Count Basiesque swing, and the floating, vaporous chords of the classic Davis/Gil Evans ensembles." Hargrove also recorded with Dallas neo-soul vocalist Erykah Badu, spurring "new fusions of jazz, soul, hip-hop and R & B that would bring eager younger listeners to jazz." Courtesy of Carl Sidle.

Born in Dallas in 1956, Drew Phelps played tuba in high school. He switched to string bass at the University of North Texas in Denton. He has recorded and/or played with Little Jack Melody, MC 900 Foot Jesus, Sara Hickman, James Clay, Nuradeen Fameen, the Quebe Sisters Band, and many others, including the Drew Phelps Group and Drew Phelps and his Electric Band. Courtesy of Carl Sidle.

Dallas multi-instrumentalist Roger Boykin (guitar, bass, piano/keyboards, flute, saxophone) is equally adept in blues, gospel, jazz, or funk. He taught at the Booker T. Washington Performing and Visual Arts High School for sixteen years. Boykin founded the Dallas label Soultex Records in 1967, and one of his symphonic works was performed by the Dallas Symphony Orchestra in 1986. His play *Zanzibar* was produced by the Black Academy of Arts and Letters in 1990, and his novel, *A Date at the Opera,* was released digitally in 2015. Courtesy of Carl Sidle.

The Fort Worth Symphony, joined by Coleman's jazz ensemble, presented the world premiere of the complete version of Ornette's composition *Skies of America*. Coleman told the press that the work had been inspired by his visit to a Native American reservation in Montana. The orchestra represented the skies and the jazz group symbolized the goings-on on the earthly plane.

The brainchild of Ed Bass, Caravan of Dreams, with its rooftop cactus garden and geodesic dome, grotto bar, theater, and restaurant was described as "the first avant-garde performing arts center architected by and for the artist and audience that enjoys the new, living and experimental in jazz, blues, theatre, dance and film." Before it closed in 2001, the unique venue hosted a remarkable variety of music and other live performance. Even *Naked Lunch* author and high priest of beatdom William Burroughs performed at the Caravan of Dreams.

Twelfth Street Rag

Ragtime, a style of music popular from about 1899 to 1917, is variously described as an important influence on jazz and as jazz's immediate precursor. And one of the most popular compositions of the genre, "Twelfth Street Rag," was written by Fort Worth piano man Euday Bowman.

After growing up on his grandparents' farm near Mansfield, Euday appears to have moved in with his sister Mary in Fort Worth. She taught him to tickle the ivories, and soon brother Bowman was playing local night spots while working by day as a junk dealer. Cheryl L. Simon noted in the Texas State Historical Association's *Handbook of Texas Music* that Bowman "probably wrote 'Twelfth Street Rag' while playing in a Main Street shoeshine parlor located between Tenth and Eleventh Streets in Fort Worth." An aunt of jazz writer Dave Oliphant often heard the composer practicing as she passed by the parlor.

With its "unusual combination of a repeating three-note melody and duple-metered bass," Simon added, the song "had a profound influence on jazz from the late 1920s through the 1940s." The piece was recorded by such seminal figures as Louis Armstrong, Duke Ellington, Fats Waller, Count Basie, Benny Goodman, Bob Wills, and Liberace. Oliphant observed that it was waxed by more artists than all of ragtime master Scott Joplin's compositions combined.

Some sources, including the all-things-historical-in-Fort Worth online blog *Hometown by Handlebar*, contend that Bowman's rag was written in Kansas City, where the piano player spent a fair amount of time, and that its title refers to a street in that city. Hometown also notes that Bowman's royalties from the song did not soar until 1948, when Pee Wee Hunt and his Orchestra recorded a version that topped the charts.

After his forty-years-in-the-making "overnight success," Bowman died in 1949. "In a final grand gesture," reports the Fort Worth blogger, "Euday Louis Bowman used his late-won fortune to erect for himself and his sister one of the grandest non-cattle-baron mausoleums at Oakwood Cemetery."

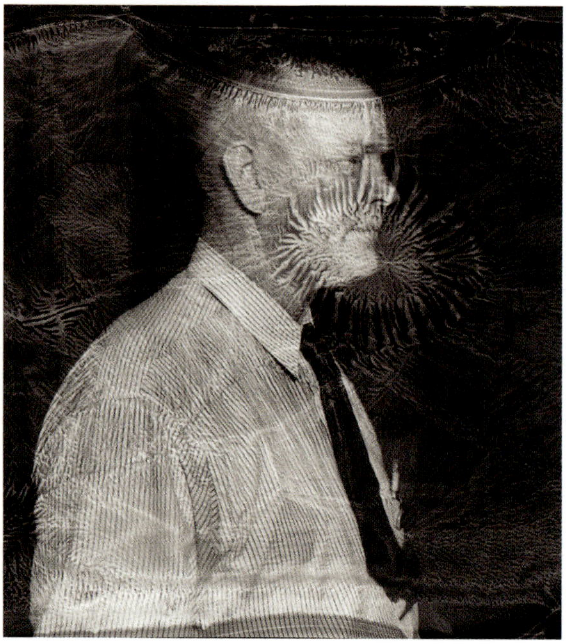

People passing by a Main Street shoeshine parlor in Fort Worth could often hear Euday Bowman practicing. Bowman may have written his widely recorded "Twelfth Street Rag" in the parlor. Portrait of Bowman from damaged 1937 negative. Courtesy of University of Texas at Arlington Special Collections.

The Adolphus Hotel reportedly hired the Alphonso Trent Orchestra after hearing the talented ensemble busking on the street in 1925. Courtesy of Sumter Bruton.

BIG Bands

Ragtime also influenced the style of music played by the big bands (or, as it's often written, Big Bands) that enjoyed its heydays in the '20s, '30s, and '40s. Generally comprising at least ten musicians with trumpet, trombone, saxophone, and rhythm sections, the big style began to form before and after World War I from a mixture of New Orleans jazz and ensemble sounds. Strains of brass band, waltz, and ragtime styles—combined with touches of West Indies rhythms and black spirituals—mingled to refine the sound through the Jazz Age of the 1920s.

Dallas and Fort Worth, of course, produced their fair share of charismatic bandleaders whose large ensembles played for dancers dressed to the nines in elegant ballrooms and swank supper clubs. Smith Ballew, Tex Beneke, and the "silver-haired daddy-o" Bobby Peters graced bandstands in Fort Worth, and over in Dallas Jack Gardner and His Orchestra and the Alphonso Trent Orchestra likely influenced a young trumpeter growing up in Forney in the 1920s and '30s named Hugh Fowler.

The Alphonso Trent Orchestra, described in publicity as "12 brown-skinned marvels," was the first African American house band at Dallas's Adolphus Hotel. According to Richard Zelade's 2015 book, *Austin in the Jazz Age*, the band was busking on the street in 1925 when the hotel "booked them for a two-week gig that lasted a year," though "the Klan threatened to tar and feather them." And according to *The Handbook of Texas Music*, the group soon became the first black ensemble in the nation to have a regular radio program, on Dallas's WFAA. Flyers claimed that Trent's "eccentric drummer," A. C. Godley, was the "originator of the drum solo." Jazz historian Ross Russell wrote that the Alphonso Trent Orchestra was "an anomaly rather than a model of Texas style . . . an eastern dance band, masquerading in high heel boots, with a Texas flavor to its music."

"Tell your friends / You'll meet them in Dallas, / In the town / Where there is no malice," urged Big D crooners in the 1915 composition, "Meet Me in Dallas." The Jack Gardner-penned tune, which was "approved by Henry D. Lindsley, mayor of Dallas," was written to influence the Democratic Party to hold its 1916 national convention in Dallas. "It is our intention / To have a big convention / And I'll expect to see you." (Alas, the DNC that year responded instead to "Meet Me in St. Louis.")

Nearly a decade later, in November of 1924, the Jack Gardner Orchestra huddled in the portable studios of OKeh Phonograph Corporation at

According to a 1925 *Dallas Morning News* article, popular bandleader Jack Gardner arrived in Dallas in 1908. His bands grew in size and acclaim until he led the house band at the Adolphus Hotel for a time, and he recorded for OKeh in Dallas in 1924 and 1925. Gardner seated at piano, with, left to right, Red Mills, Ralph Brown, Bob Dean, unidentified, Stanton Crocker, Herman Waldman, Bob Harris, Lou Harris, Bob Blasingame. Courtesy of Pat Bywaters.

Courtesy of Pat Bywaters.

Courtesy of Pat Bywaters.

Long before Glenn Miller gave Gordon "Tex" Beneke his Lone Star nickname and Beneke's vocals and sax became renowned in songs like "Chattanooga Choo Choo" and "Kalamazoo," the Fort Worth native and Paschal High grad would ride the Interurban down to Cleburne and then ride in Harvey Anderson Sr.'s car to Glen Rose, where he played with Anderson's band at the Oakdale Casino. Beneke (left) joined the Miller band in 1938 and became the leader after Miller disappeared during the war in 1944. After Tex led the famous band, another Fort Worth musician took over, Ray McKinley. A 1940 issue of *Metronome* said of Tex, "He plays the sort of tenor you smile at the minute you hear it.... It's full of color and depth, light and shade, soul and body." Courtesy of University of Texas at Arlington Special Collections

1917 Main Street in downtown Dallas to lay down some tracks. Texas music historian Andrew Brown has observed that these sessions, which also included recordings by the Chenoweth Cornfield Symphony Orchestra, were the first commercial recordings in the state.

"Looking Legs Over Is His Business," read the headline of a lengthy 1925 *Dallas Morning News* piece on Gardner. The piano-playing bandleader explained that he watched feet at dances to see if his music was "getting over" with the crowd. Gardner told the reporter that he was born in Toronto (other sources say Joliet, Illinois) and that he gained his first professional experience with a trio while still a little tyke. "It was with a three-piece combination," Gardner recalled. "A man about 70 years old played fiddle, a big negro played cello, and I played organ."

His father did not approve of music as a career, so young Jack ran away with a traveling theater troupe. The thespians got stranded on railroad tracks just north of Dallas when their manager disappeared. As Gardner told the reporter, he made his way to a nearby town, where he proclaimed to a dance teacher that he was "the best pianist in the world" and began playing for classes. The teacher, Gardner recalled, told him that he was not so hot. "I profited a lot by his instruction," the bandleader confided. "One idea I gained, which I know is true, is that the music for a dance should be played so it goes out over the floor and spreads outward and upward."

Traveling the state for a couple of years and playing for dance classes, Gardner continued, he came to Dallas in 1908, liked the city, and stayed. His Jack Gardner Trio debuted in 1913.

The ensemble grew in pieces, with several name changes, including Jack Gardner's Supersyncopating Six Orchestra. By 1925, it was nine pieces, including banjo, tuba, and violin. The orchestra began an extended run at the Adolphus Hotel that December.

To kick off the Adolphus association, and to celebrate the first anniversary of his recording career, the local OKeh distributor announced it would present free copies of Gardner's records to each couple attending the hotel dances. The dozen-plus sides, the distributor stated, were all "typically 'Gardneresque' in lilt, catchiness, and entrancing melody." The Adolphus joined in, presenting each couple with the Gardner tune, "Dallas, I Love You," though it's unclear if the hotel gifted a recording or the song's sheet music.

Another "jazz band" that recorded when the traveling OKeh studio returned to Big D in the fall of 1925, Jimmie's Joys, also became wildly popular in Dallas-Fort Worth. The Joys had a slogan on their bass drum: "If you don't dance, get on and ride!" Sherman-raised Smith Ballew played banjo with the Joys for a time. A faded 1923 *Star-Telegram* photo depicts the seven-piece outfit preparing for a radio concert on WBAP and a performance at Meadowmere Country Club. Later that year, the young banjoist and singer formed his own ensemble, the Texajazzers. And as the Fort Worth history blog *Hometown by Handlebar* points out, in 1926, Ballew's orchestra was the house band at the Fort Worth Club. Later in the Roaring Twenties, Glenn Miller joined Ballew's band on trombone. In the '30s Ballew had a career in Hollywood horse operas, and in the '50s he was back in Fort Worth working in PR for Convair and General Dynamics.

Another grainy newspaper photograph depicts the 1924 iteration of the Fort Worth Recreation Board's Junior Orchestra, a twelve-piece outfit that included ten-year-old Gordon Beneke on saxophone. In 1936, as a member of the Ben Young Band, he played the Fort Worth Frontier Centennial Exposition. A few years later, he joined the Glenn Miller Orchestra. When he strolled into rehearsal, Miller quipped, "Hello there, Texas, whaddya say?" The banter soon became a fixture of the show, and "Gordon" was soon replaced by "Tex." Tex Beneke lent his horn to Miller classics like "In the Mood" and his Texas drawl-inflected vocals to standards like "Chattanooga Choo-Choo" and "I've Got a Gal in Kalamazoo." After Glenn Miller joined the air force and disappeared on a flight from London to France in late 1944, Tex fronted the band for several years at the request of the Miller estate.

Other metroplex big bands included Jan Garber, Phil Baxter, Harris Brothers' Texans, Frensley Moore's Black and Gold Serenaders, Fred Cahoon, Russell Ward, Denny Beckner, and many more. The leader of Chief Gonzales's Texas Hotel Orchestra in Fort Worth is said to have been a Native American.

Pappy Dolsen's first Dallas nightclub, La Boheme, opened in 1924 with a five-piece jazz band. "A kid named Pork Chops danced and played music on a Prince Albert can gadget," said Pappy in 1967. During Prohibition, the club "bought the best Freestone County whiskey in half-gallon jars." Pappy's legendary Showland on West Commerce in Oak Cliff was a landmark of Big D nightlife from 1946 to 1958. Courtesy of Joe Whitney.

Courtesy of George Gimarc.

Sonora native Gene Baugh served as music director of WBAP from 1931 to 1949. Before locating in Fort Worth, he led a band at the Baker Hotel in Mineral Wells. A cellist, he was also on the faculty of Texas Wesleyan University. Here, Baugh's orchestra graces the ballroom stage in what appears to be Fort Worth's Blackstone Hotel. Left to right: rear, Bobby Turley, Fay "Smitty" Smith, possibly Dave Singletary. Front, Teddy Graves, probably Marius Thor, George Orum, unidentified, Ann Shipp, Red Woodward, Ken McGarrity, two unidentified. WBAP staff guitarist Smitty Smith played on Ernest Tubb's first recording of "Walking the Floor Over You." Courtesy of University of Texas at Arlington Special Collections.

Dallas native and pianist Vincent "Jelly" Parrino toured with John Philip Sousa's band during World War I. In 1929 his own band, described as "a very peppy organization," played "the latest popular fox-trots and waltzes," including tunes like "Digga Digga Do," "Shreveport Sob," "Four or Five Times," and "Washboard Blues." Left to right: Robert Sparkman, Johnnie Strange, Frank Drobil, Vincent Parrino, Dean Parrino, Norman Pickett, Happy Brooks, John Lowry, and Hal Baker. Circa 1927. For years before his death in 1984, reedman Baker led a popular jazz band at Dallas's Greenville Ave. Bar & Grill. Courtesy of Steve Parrino.

Active for decades, Durward J. Cline formed his orchestra while attending SMU. The opulent Club Bagdad in Grand Prairie opened shortly before the economic crash of 1929 and operated until 1945. Its lavish Middle Eastern motif included a $10,000 silk ceiling canopy imported from Istanbul. In 1947, the film *Juke Joint* was partly filmed in South Dallas and at the Bagdad. Its score was composed by popular Dallas bandleader Red Calhoun. Fellow saxman Buddy Tate, a native of Sherman, said that if Red Calhoun and his Dallas Swingers had moved to New York, the Big D artist "really could have made a name for himself." Summer 1929. Left to right: Willard Cox, Vernon Reed, Wilbur Ard, unidentified, Tom Nash, Durward Cline, Jimmy McManus, Red Wingert, Dick Richardson, Abe Chesney. Courtesy of Griffith Osborn.

Edgar Russell's Foot Warmers jazzed up Dallas in the Roaring Twenties, playing "the most rhythmic ragtime music of the present day," including such tunes as "Wild Jazz," "Muscle Shoals Blues," "Got to Cool My Doggies Now," and "Twelfth Street Rag." Left to right: J. Eldridge Eastland (a.k.a. "Puss," "Jimmy," or "Scat"), trombone; Jack Russell, banjo; Ed Russell, drums; Ted Parrino, piano; Abe Ackenhausen, sax; Rufus Bennett, sax. Courtesy of Steve Parrino.

Dallas resident Hugh Fowler started his first dance orchestra while still in high school in 1939. This photo, circa late 1940s/early '50s, predated the era of his larger big band of twelve or more pieces. Courtesy of Gene Fowler.

Abe Weinstein opened his first Dallas nightspot, a "dime-a-dance place" called the Triangle Club, in 1933. "But the city passed an ordinance against the place," said Abe in 1972, when Abe's thirty-five-year-old Colony Club was demolished. When the Colony started in 1938, it was called Abe and Pappy's before Abe bought out partner Pappy Dolsen. During the war, American sailors renamed their battleship Abe & Pappy's. "Everybody, everywhere, seemed to know about us," said Abe. Courtesy of Gene Fowler.

The swank expanse of the Colony Club interior. Courtesy of Sumter Bruton.

There have doubtless been many "jazz centers of the South," and Big D had its own in the Pink Poodle. Courtesy of George Gimarc.

Courtesy of the Portal to Texas History.

Like many of the legendary night spots on the Jacksboro Highway—a.k.a. Thunder Road—the Rocket and the Skyliner hosted a variety of musical acts. Courtesy of Ted Tucker.

Known as the "Silver-Haired Daddyo," hipster bandleader Bobby Peters also had two popular shows on WBAP-TV before his death at age forty-eight in 1961. Like many Fort Worth big bands, he often played the Rocket Club on the Jacksboro Highway. The shot of Daddyo on a miniature pony is from his TV show, *Bobby Peters Jamboree*. Courtesy of Trinity River Music.

Jimmy Rovitto (left) played sax for the FW Air Force band at Carswell, and he was also proficient on violin, piano, organ, and accordion. In World War II, he participated in the Normandy invasion and the Battle of the Bulge. After the war, he had a popular radio program and formed a five-piece band, playing country clubs, hotels, and upscale nightclubs. In the above photo, the group played for what became President John F. Kennedy's last breakfast, at the Texas Hotel, on November 22, 1963. "I'll remember that dark day forever," Rovitto said. Courtesy of James Rovitto Jr.

Courtesy of James Rovitto Jr.

Born in Dallas in 1985, Matt Tolentino grew up playing the clarinet and never missing an episode of *The Lawrence Welk Show* on TV. He added tuba, saxophone, and accordion to his instruments, and after high school toured with a South Texas polka band, the Sauerkrauts. Then he played accordion and bass sax with an Austin band, the White Ghost Shivers. Around 2007 he started a big band called the Singapore Slingers, with a repertoire that includes a musical hybrid from the late 1910s and early 1920s called "rag-a-jazz." He also heads a smaller outfit, the Matt Tolentino Band. Courtesy of Matt Tolentino.

To the baby boomer generation, of course, big band music had largely been the less exciting sound of their parents' youth. That changed somewhat with a revival of big band popularity in the 1990s. And interestingly, generational conflict fueled by clashes in musical taste has not been limited to the rock 'n' roll era. Having had a brief period of estrangement from his own big band leader father in the 1960s, for reasons stemming from aesthetic preferences, Gene Fowler was surprised to learn, when writing a magazine article about the big band revival around 2000, that his parents' and grandparents' generations experienced similar cultural turbulence.

"In the 1930s," Central Texas bandleader Ken Ragsdale told Gene, "you had two types of dance bands, sweet and swing." Sweet bands, such as Dallas's Jan Garber, created a more sedate sound of romantic orchestral ballads. Swing bands, like that of Texan Harry James, played a jazz-oriented music that, well, swung.

Benny Goodman introduced the swing style in 1934 on a cross-country tour from New York to Los Angeles. At first, the new sound left audiences cold, and ballroom operators said it was too loud. By the time Goodman and company hit LA, however, the crowds went wild. In his 1964 book *The Wonderful Era of the Great Dance Bands*, Leo Walker calls the Goodman innovation "the single greatest event . . . in the whole history of American popular dance music."

"But swing was controversial when it first hit," added Ken Ragsdale. "Magazines and newspapers editorialized against it—one columnist warned that young people's addiction to swing would prove as disastrous to their minds and bodies as drugs and alcohol."

Hugh Fowler's scrapbook made clear which side of the equation drove his rhythmic muse. Anytime an ad for an engagement of his dance orchestra appeared near an ad for a Harry James gig, that clipping went in the book, with the James ad included.

And Jack Gardner shot down the idea "that the youth of today are wilder than any other generation and that they are jazz-mad" a full decade before the advent of swing. "I hear a lot of talk about 'jellybeans' and 'flappers' but for the life of me I can't tell you what a jellybean is," he told the *Dallas Morning News* in 1925. "They are all kids and putting on a pair of big-legged trousers doesn't make a boy any different. There is no cause to worry over the younger generation, from what I have seen of them."

After graduating from TCU with a business degree, jazz and big band drummer Sumter Bruton (technically he was Sumter Bruton Jr.) opened the venerable Fort Worth store Record Town in 1957, a shop that influenced generations of area musicians and music fans. The left-handed drummer performed with a who's who of local musicians before his death in 1988. From 1962 to 1967 he kept the beat for a trio with Jim Ecker and John Hawkins at Casa del Sol. He also played with bands led by pianist George Campbell, whose ensembles often included guitarist Charlie Carey and trumpeter Curly Broyles. In 1986, Campbell expanded his band to a dozen pieces to play his fiftieth reunion at Paschal High School, adding local artists like J. B. Brinkley and Betty Rose. The idea was to re-create the same musical program performed by the school's musicians back in 1936.
Courtesy of Sumter Bruton.

Courtesy of Sumter Bruton.

Ernest Tubb spent two very important years in Fort Worth, from 1940 to 1942. For much of that time, he traveled Texas, performing on town squares and grocery store parking lots as the Gold Chain Troubadour for Gold Chain Flour. Courtesy of Johnny Case and Tracy Pitcox.

CHAPTER EIGHT

Country-Western

Kindly Keep It Country...Western

Ernest Tubb hitchhiked into Fort Worth from San Angelo in November of 1940. Skinny as a gangly mesquite, the twenty-seven-year-old singer landed a six-days-a-week radio show on KGKO. And in the two years that he lived in the town where Amon Carter said the West begins, Tubb saw his popularity skyrocket as his musical idiom shifted into a modernized honky-tonk sound.

Hillbillies and singing cowboys filled the radio waves and recording studios of the twenties and thirties. In the forties, the two forms of American folk music merged into country and western. And Ellis County native Ernest Tubb represents the transition perhaps better than any other artist. On November 28, 1940, station listings carried "Range ballads by the popular KGKO newcomer, Cowboy Tubb!" In early '41, *Star-Telegram* readers got a heads-up on Tubb's vernacular performance style: "Cowboy Tubb was a student of the late Jimmy Rogers [sic], the famed singing brakeman. You'll surely enjoy Tubb's tuneful songs and guitar playing without benefit of tuning fork or pitch pipe." A few days later, it was noted that KGKO's "cowboy singer" played Rodgers's "own custom-made guitar."

Ernest Tubb got a job on KGKO shortly after arriving in Fort Worth in November 1940. First called "Cowboy Tubb" in radio listings, he soon became the "Smiling Troubadour." Courtesy of Johnny Case.

Ernest Tubb had begun developing his own style after having his tonsils removed in 1939, which forced him to cease attempting to replicate Jimmie Rodgers's distinctive vocals. Without his tonsils, he could no longer yodel. Distraught at first, he thought about suing the doctor for botching the operation. But in time, Tubb's post-op voice became a warm, familiar landmark in the American grain. *Houston Post* music writer Bob Claypool described it as "a strange, unmusical timbre that chugs along in a loping, craggy fashion and then—at the end of each lyric line—slides one quarter tone off pitch."

By late February 1941, listings had begun to lose the "cowboy balladeer" angle, instead focusing

Ernest Tubb onstage at Fort Worth's Panther Hall. Legendary radio personality and songwriter Bill Mack, a.k.a. the "Midnight Cowboy," at far left, hosted the *Cowtown Jamboree*. Courtesy of the Wittliff Collections, Texas State University.

on the twenty-seven-year-old singer as Texas's "smiling troubadour." In one broadcast, a live remote from the new home of Margo's Shoe Store on Houston Street, Tubb teamed up for a "dazzling musical show" with the Texas Cowgirls, popular KGKO artists described as "radio's most famous all-girl string band" and "five lovely ladies playing and singing the songs of the West." In May 1941, alliterative copywriters went wild, announcing that "Tuneful Tubb, the torrid Texas troubadour, will inquire vocally, 'Are You Tired of Me, Darling?'"

The romantic melancholy implied by the song's title had hold of Ernest that spring. Partly motivated by marital strain, his then-wife Elaine took the kids and went to visit her parents in San Antonio. Alone and pacing in their Fort Worth apartment, Tubb jotted down one of his greatest songs in twenty minutes. And when Decca Records producer Dave Kapp asked the singer to come to Dallas and record some sides that April, the first of the eight tunes Tubb recorded at Big D's Biggs Studio was the newly composed, destined-to-be-a-classic "Walking the Floor Over You."

The Dallas Decca session also marked the first time Tubb utilized an electric guitar on a recording. According to Ronnie Pugh's 1996 biography, *Ernest Tubb: The Texas Troubadour*, a Fort Worth jukebox operator told Tubb that he needed to pump up the volume on his records because when the crowd started getting loud, people quit playing Tubb records and instead punched the buttons for tunes by bigger bands like Bob Wills. Thus, for the Dallas session, Tubb recruited Fay "Smitty" Smith, who played electric guitar with the Red Hawks, a WBAP staff band.

In June 1941, Tubb became KGKO's Gold Chain Troubadour, sponsored by Universal Mills, makers of Gold Chain Flour. The company provided him with a new Plymouth outfitted with a loudspeaker on the roof and painted with company slogans. For the next eighteen months or so—with time off in August 1942 to appear in the Hollywood movie *Fighting Buckaroo*—Tubb toured Fort Worth and North Texas grocery stores and town squares, performing on-the-spot concerts sponsored by Gold Chain Flour.

By October 1942 it had become apparent that Ernest Tubb was destined for national stardom, and Gold Chain graciously tore up his contract with its modest remuneration. Tubb soon moved on to Nashville. Among the throngs of Texans who missed the plainspoken voice that managed to somehow sound upbeat while singing even the saddest of songs was young Willie Nelson in Abbott, just north of Waco.

In 1955, at the age of twenty-two, Willie headed for Fort Worth, where he landed a deejay job on the country-western station KCNC. He did the job the Willie way, of course, playing his guitar and singing along to the tunes he spun. According to Joe Nick Patoski's 2008 biography, *Willie Nelson: An Epic Life*, shoppers at the downtown Leonard Brothers Department Store could sometimes catch the young "Red Headed Stranger" performing live in weekend remotes from the furniture department.

The sidewalk in front of Leonard's would later provide the setting for Nelson's melancholic Christmas song, "Pretty Paper," about a man with a disability who sold pencils and wrapping paper. The song was first recorded by Roy Orbison in 1963, but as Bud Kennedy wrote in the *Fort Worth Star-Telegram*, the man's identity was a mystery until 2016. His name was Frankie Brierton, and he lived in the Palo Pinto County hamlet of Santo until his death in 1973 at the age of seventy-four. Brierton's legs had been weakened by childhood spinal meningitis. "He crept on all fours along Houston or Throckmorton streets outside Leonards," wrote Kennedy, "wearing chunky gloves and kneepads made from old tire tread and a custom leather vest with a pencil rack and coin box sewn into the back."

Nelson left Fort Worth in 1956 for the Northwest but was back in the city where the West begins by 1958. He got a job playing guitar on the *Cowtown Hoedown*, which was broadcast from the Majestic Theater over radio station KCUL and rebroadcast on the powerful Mexican border station XEG located in Monterrey, Nuevo Leon. The *Hoedown*'s Uncle Hank Craig, who arranged the hookup with XEG (mailing address Fort Worth, 11, Texas), became Willie's manager for a time and got him signed to D Records. So Willie Nelson's first recordings with his own vocals were made in Fort Worth.

The "Still Is Still Movin' to Me" songwriter headed for Houston in 1959, and by 1961 he had landed in Nashville, where he was recruited to play bass in Ray Price's Cherokee Cowboys. According to Rich Kienzle's 2003 book, *Southwest*

While working as a Fort Worth deejay in the 1950s, Willie dreamed of playing the joints along the Jacksboro Highway. In '55, the "Red Headed Stranger" and the Dumplin' Eaters (best band name ever!) graced the stage at the Morehead Club. Courtesy of Trinity River Music.

The downtown Fort Worth Majestic Theater, where the *Cowtown Hoedown* (which was sometimes also called the *Cowtown Jamboree)* took place. Courtesy of George Gimarc.

A great lineup of *Jamboree* guests and 1950s Dallas talent. Left to right: Dewey Groom, Billy Walker, Luke Wills, Lefty Frizzell, Charlie Duff, Riley Crabtree, T. Texas Tyler, Ray Price. Courtesy of David Dennard.

Regulars on the *Saturday Night Shindig*. Standing, left to right: Jimmy Kelley, Joe Bill, Al Turner, Bill Noble, unidentified. Kneeling, left to right: Bobby Williamson, unidentified, Leon Rhodes, Billy Jack Saucier. Courtesy of Kevin Coffey.

Shuffle, Price graduated from Dallas's Adamson High School in 1942. He first sang publicly after service in the Marines during World War Two.

After the war, Price was enrolled in North Texas Agricultural College (now the University of Texas at Arlington) with plans to become a veterinarian. But one night at Roy's House Café in Dallas, he "sat in" for a song, on vocals, with some musician friends. Eventually, a break on Abilene's *Hillbilly Circus* led to a slot on the *Big "D" Jamboree* in 1949. He recorded some demos at Jim Beck's studio in Dallas, where he met and became friends with Lefty Frizzell, which led to a recording contract with Nashville's Bullet Records. Lefty recorded his landmark honky-tonker "If You've Got the Money I've Got the Time" at Beck's in July 1950.

Fort Worth native Roger Miller also logged some time as a Cherokee Cowboy. Guitarist Leon Rhodes, who began playing professionally in Dallas at age sixteen, played with both Price and Frizzell, and he was in the house band at Jack Ruby's Silver Spur and Bob Wills Ranch House in 1960, when he was lured away to join Ernest Tubb's Texas Troubadours.

Countless other musicians played for the thriving country-western scene in Dallas-Fort Worth in the '40s, '50s, and '60s. For the most part, though, so long as they had an audience and got paid, they probably didn't care if you called it hillbilly, country, country-western, or whatever. And all those terms continued to be used. Way back in 1926, Ed Scanlan and his Coon Hunters from Clear Creek provided "old-fashioned country music" on WFAA's *Farmer's Hour*. And though Steve Sholes was in charge of RCA Victor's "country-western department" in 1954, as he told *Dallas Morning News* entertainment writer Paul Rosenfield, "You can't sell western music anymore. In fact, most of the former cowboy stars have changed to the country style of song and singing."

"I can tell you exactly what happened," said cowboy culture ambassador Red Steagall in 2005, when asked why the western part of country music went *thataway*. "I was chairman of the board of the Academy of Country and Western Music in 1968 when everyone on the board, except for me, voted to remove 'and Western' from the Academy's name. Except for Marty Robbins, it was devastating to western music."

Owner of the Ole Top Rail country-western club in Dallas, and KSKY deejay, Slim McDonald coproduced the Texas State Barn Dance at the Sportatorium in 1947. Courtesy of George Gimarc.

Big D Jamboree

"DI-RECT from Ed McLemore's Sportatorium at the corner of Cadiz and Industrial boulevards in downtown big friendly Dallas . . . the home of professional wrestling on Tuesday night and the home of the Hillbillies on Saturday night. . . . We've got bass fiddle players, big fiddle players, little fiddle players, middle-sized fiddle players, and the doggonedest bunch of singers you ever saw in your life . . . pickin' and singin' from the real early evenin' until real late at night."

Delivered with down-home flair by emcees like Johnny Hicks and Big Al Turner, those words introduced Texas's most popular "barn dance" program, the *Big "D" Jamboree*. From the late 1940s to the mid-1960s, the *Jamboree* provided an important venue for both regional and nationally known artists. And fans flocked to the show. "We'd pack that place with 5,000 people every Saturday night," recalled Johnny Hicks shortly before his death in 1997. Thousands more tuned in to the program on radio and TV.

Big D Jamboree cast, 1949. Standing (from left): Marvin and Charlie Morris, Otis West, Riley Crabtree, Billy Jack Saucier, Red Gilliam, Al Turner, Tony Miller, Ray Munroe, Buddy Griffin, Roy Wiley, Billy Walker (in his Tall Texan mask). Kneeling (from left): Gene O'Quin, Bobby Williamson, Barbara Hazzard, Betty Lou Lobb, Buster White. Courtesy of the Buddy Griffin Collection, Kevin Coffey, and David Dennard.

Jamboree artists hit the road, 1955. Standing, Marvin Montgomery, Carroll Hubbard, Paul Blunt. Kneeling, Douglas Bragg, Tex Raye, Charline Arthur, Joe Bill. Courtesy of David Dennard.

Orville Couch won a spot on *Saturday Night Shindig* in 1953, then joined the *Jamboree* after *Shindig* ended in late 1954. A native of Ferris, where his parents ran a crossroads country store, Couch told reporters that his father would stand him on the store counter to perform when he was "just a little shaver." Describing his style, he said he just "rears back and lets her fly." Courtesy of George Gimarc.

Raised in Mount Pleasant, *Jamboree* regular Riley Crabtree survived polio to become a regional star with records like "Shackles and Chains" and "Lonely World." According to the *Handbook of Texas Music,* Crabtree turned down membership on the *Grand Ole Opry* to remain in Dallas where he supplemented his music income with work as an auto mechanic to support his family. Shown here with longtime *Jamboree* announcer Johnny Hicks. Courtesy of David Dennard.

The Lovett Sisters, Colleen and Char, began singing as kids with their dad Joe, leader of the Dallas-based big band The Southern Syncopaters. "We remember all-night jam sessions in our living room," said the sisters, "with our daddy singing and playing the guitar and our mother cooking up bacon and eggs for the group. We thought everyone lived that way and we loved it!" The sisters were still attending an Oak Cliff high school when they debuted on *Saturday Night Shindig* and got signed to Imperial Records. Some of the tunes they recorded were written by their grandmother, Eva Burke. Courtesy of David Dennard.

"Groovy" Joe Poovey, who also performed as Johnny Dallas, was one of many *Jamboree* acts who straddled country-western and rockabilly styles. Courtesy of David Dennard.

Dallas musician David Dennard turned culture detective in the 1990s, hunting for vintage *Jamboree* audio. Though it was widely believed that its sound lingered only in memory, Dennard found forty-nine *Jamboree* tracks on sixteen-inch transcription discs at the Library of Congress. The programs had been broadcast overseas by the US Armed Services. The persistent researcher also found four tracks in Taylor, Texas, that had belonged to *Jamboree* guest performer Jimmie Heap. Dennard produced and released several CDs of the material through his independent Dallas label, Dragon Street Records.

"From the beginning," wrote Kevin Coffey in one of the CD booklets, "the show was notable, in an area otherwise best known as a hot bed of western swing . . . for being instead a clearly 'hillbilly' show that eschewed such uptown sounds for more straightforward country sounds." Guest stars ranged from Hank Williams to Elvis Presley, and the revolving local cast featured artists such as the Light Crust Doughboys, Charline Arthur, Riley Crabtree, Helen Hall, and Sid King & The Five Strings.

Other metroplex barn dance programs of the post-war era include *Saturday Night Shindig*, which broadcast from the Fair Park Band Shell on Dallas's WFAA. The show followed the barn dance formula of a local cast with featured guests. When Patsy Montana visited in 1954, for instance, the "regular cast" included Sonny James, Bobby Williamson, Bob Shelton, Neal Jones, Ralph Sanford, Orville Couch, LaFawn Paul, Jimmy Kelley, and Paul Buskirk.

Fort Worth, of course, had the *Cowtown Hoedown*. And in the 1960s and early '70s, the *Cowtown Jamboree* aired live on Fort Worth TV from Panther Hall, a giant honky-tonk that rivaled the Longhorn Ballroom. Willie Nelson recorded a live album there in 1966. *Cowtown Jamboree* capped off a Saturday afternoon and early evening of c&w viewing on Fort Worth station KTVT that included *Gospel Singing Jubilee*, *Cowboy Weaver*, *The Porter Wagoner Show*, *Buck Owens*, *The Wilburn Brothers Show*, and *The Ernest Tubb Show*.

"The show we all waited for," recalled *Rockzilla* webzine blogger Michael Johnson around 2002, "was *Cowtown Jamboree*. . . . It would be fantastic if someone would discover recordings of those shows. EVERYBODY played Panther Hall. We got to see Willie Nelson, George Jones, Lawton Williams, and Daddy's favorite Purty Little Miss Wanda Jackson. Bob Wills was on *Cowtown Jamboree* many times. I remember seeing Leon McAuliffe play 'Steel Guitar Rag,' and Bob with that big cigar and that grin. It would be hard to name a country star alive at that time who didn't play Panther Hall."

Hailing from Greenville, the Belew Twins, Bobby and Benny, became *Jamboree* regulars after winning a Search for Talent contest. At times, the comic part of the youngsters' act even included drag performances. Courtesy of David Dennard.

Growing up in Dallas, Jimmy Fautheree was encouraged to go into showbiz by his parents. As he told Andrew Brown, "My daddy used to say, 'Boy, you ain't never gonna get nowhere 'til you learn to play that blues'....I'd go to downtown Dallas....listen to the colored people play on the sidewalks of Deep Elm." Though Fautheree became a *Louisiana Hayride* regular, he often returned to the Big D to guest on the *Jamboree*. Courtesy of Carol Galt.

Charley Pride Mows the Lawn

Shortly after Charley Pride moved to Dallas and bought a home in the suburbs in 1969 (or in the early '70s by other accounts), he was mowing his lawn one day when a neighbor came over and, assuming he was a handyman, asked him to mow her lawn because she was having a party. Charley said he would be glad to and got right on it. Soon, the lady's husband, better versed in country-western stars, arrived home and asked, "Honey, why is Charley Pride mowing our lawn?"

That story is urban country music folklore, but if it were true, it would be handily emblematic

Charley Pride first heard country-western sounds while growing up in Mississippi, when his sharecropper father would tune in the Grand Ole Opry from Nashville. Pride relocated to Dallas in the early 1970s, after patiently defying the genre's racial barriers in the mid-1960s. Courtesy of the Wittliff Collections, Texas State University.

As former Texas Music Office director Casey Monahan told the *Star-Telegram*'s Shirley Jinkins, "Fort Worth's Panther Hall had a long and illustrious reign, from 1963 to 1978, as the World's Largest Honky Tonk." Courtesy of Ted Tucker.

of the affable determination Pride deployed to rise to the top of a genre sometimes thought of as "white man's soul music." The singer's considerable personal charisma went a long way towards deflating the awkwardness white audiences felt as he strode onstage early in his career. And Pride, who chose Dallas because its central location made touring easier, has maintained that he never encountered any "Jackie Robinson type" resistance in the country-western world.

The same was not true for Artie Morris from Central Texas, who tried to break the Nashville color line a decade or so before Pride. When Morris won a *Big D Jamboree* new artist competition and earned a guest shot on the show, they mistook him for a janitor when he appeared at the Sportatorium stage door.

Thunder Road

"Tonight, I'm gonna show you Fort Worth," said Willie Nelson to Johnny Bush when the Bushes trekked to Cowtown to visit the Nelsons in 1955. The first place they went, Bush wrote in his 2007 autobiography, *Whiskey River*, was the Crystal Springs Ballroom. Bush doesn't list any other venues in the foursome's Fort Worth bar crawl, but in the '50s and '60s metroplex honky-tonkers enjoyed a lot of choice.

In Dallas, Jack Ruby offered hillbilly swing and neon weepers at his Silver Spur and his Bob Wills Ranch House, later known as the Longhorn Ballroom. Al Dexter poured some of his profits from his mega-hit "Pistol Packin' Mama" into his Bridgeport Club on South Lamar and Al Dexter's Barn near the Longhorn (which became Rosa's Barn when Al and his wife divorced). When Dexter played a Grand Ole Opry package show at the North Texas Fair held at Arlington Downs, Red Foley introduced Al as "the boy who made his first guitar with a tomato box and his first million from 'Pistol Packin' Mama.'" Though *Life* magazine called the song "a national earache," it was so popular that the Duke of Windsor was heard humming its tune on a visit to the White House.

Both Dallas and Fort Worth featured a Roundup Club with c&w music. Rosa Dexter headed over to Cowtown, fronting Rosa and Her HAPPY HILLBILLIES at Stella's Dine and Dance on E. Belknap, which eventually became Rosa's Western Club. Other Tarrant County honky-tonks included Todd's Western Lounge on Exchange

Al Dexter's landmark 1936 tune, "Honky Tonk Blues," is regarded by many historians as the first c&w recording to use the term honky-tonk. But his huge 1943 hit, "Pistol Packin' Mama," inspired by a scene Dexter witnessed in the East Texas oil fields, sold millions. The peppy number became a crossover hit for Bing Crosby, the Andrews Sisters, and other artists, and the New York Yankees adopted it as their marching tune for a time. Courtesy of Pat Bywaters.

Kessler Stage Show To Present Al Dexter

Al Dexter, composer of "Pistol Packing Mama," will be the guest of Dewey Groom and his Texas Playboys Wednesday on the stage at the Kessler Theater. Groom and his band appear daily, Monday through Friday, with their "Liberty Hayloft" show from 1 to 1:30 p.m., Jimmy Wakely will be their guest on Thursday.

Dexter appeared often on the *Big D Jamboree* and other DFW venues. Here, he shares the bill with Dewey Groom at the Kessler Theater in 1948, long before the Oak Cliff moviehouse owned by Gene Autry was reborn as one of Texas's best listening rooms. Courtesy of Trinity River Music.

Cecil Luna's Rhythm Kings, seen here onstage at Dallas's Roundup Club, enjoyed a long nightly run at the South Ervay honky-tonk in the '40s and '50s. A 1952 billing cited Luna's "new 9-piece swing band featuring the famous twin fiddlers." Dub Dickerson, the singer credited with biting off a hunk of Jack Ruby's ear, often handled vocals for the Kings. Left to right: George Uptmor, Bob Jenkins, Buddy Brady, Gene Crabb, Cecil Luna, Freddy Powers, Harold Carmack, Bob Meadows. Courtesy of Kevin Coffey.

Clubs like the Roundup were strictly c&w. Courtesy of Trinity River Music.

We haven't been able to identify this lively crew, except we believe the guitarist far right is George Petton. Courtesy of Deborah Petton Bell.

In this iteration of the Paradise Ramblers, Veda Mae "Margie" Spoon is on steel, Ray Chaney is at the microphone, Johnny Strawn on fiddle, and Frankie Kinman is the seated lead guitarist. Drummer unknown. Club Paradise was on the Mansfield Highway. Courtesy of Phil Strawn.

and Jimmy's Westland Club on 80 West. Popular musician Ray Chaney opened the Stagecoach Inn in the Stockyards in 1961 and a year or two later moved it to the former Crystal Springs Ballroom. When that historic structure burned in 1967, he moved the club to a former Safeway grocery store on East Belknap, where it continues today as the Stagecoach Ballroom. When Chaney died in a 1972 auto accident at the age of forty-four, *Star-Telegram* country-western columnist Lawton Williams remembered him as "one of the most liked and respected personalities in country music," noting that his recently released album, *I've Already Been Here Too Long*, was "one of the best of the year."

But the liveliest nightlife strip in Tarrant County had to be the notorious Jacksboro Highway, also known as Thunder Road. Historian and folklorist Lonn Taylor, who recalls that fellow Fort Worth teens dared each other to venture to what they called "Jaxbeer Highway" on a Saturday night, reported on Marfa Public Radio that 3.5 miles of the strip equalled "the most dangerous road in Texas . . . notorious for shootings, stabbings, parking lot fights, and the occasional gangland killing."

Some of the swankier Thunder Road nightspots, like the Skyliner Supper Club and the Casino Ballroom, offered dancing to big bands. Delbert McClinton, Ray Sharpe, and other R & B and rockabilly stars also played Thunder Road. Fort Worth radio announcer Lee Woodward accompanied a young Willie Nelson to Jacksboro Highway country-western bars that had nicknames like the Bloody Bucket and the County Dump, with chicken wire strung in front of the bandstand to protect the musicians from flying beer bottles.

"They were rough places," Woodward told Joe Nick Patoski, "but Willie would act like he'd entered Valhalla. His eyes would get wide and he'd say, 'One of these days, I'm going to be playing here.'"

Dixie Harper, in the elaborate Western shirt, her manager, and her band onstage at Stella's Club in Fort Worth. Researcher Kevin Coffey says this version of Dixie's band may be the Blue Bonnet Brats. Kevin identifies the bass player as Ray Yates, the drummer as David Brown, the steel player as Jake Guhl, the fiddler as Cleon Kee, and the gent standing far right as Blackie Brinkley, father of popular musician J. B. Brinkley. Courtesy of Ted Tucker.

Jimmy Capps and his Country Boys were regulars at Crystal Springs, as were Charlie Mitchell and the Southern Stars. Courtesy of Jimmy Capps Jr.

Promoting a 1950 performance by Ted Daffan and his Texans at the Westland Club, on the Weatherford Highway, the *Fort Worth Star-Telegram* noted, "Daffan has been numbered among the top 10 hillbillies in the nation, and with their following—that's not hay." The article mentioned Daffan's hits like "Truck Drivers' Blues," "Born to Lose," and "No Letter Today," plus a new one, "Got $5 and It's Saturday Night." The reporter also commented, "Daffan leads a quiet life in Arlington, where he's lived for four years. He flies to Hollywood to make his recordings." Ten years earlier, a snootier scribe for the *Dallas Morning News,* under the headline, "Bands on Wax," observed, "Two disks on the hillbilly side are getting a very strong play. They are 'New San Antonio Rose' (Okeh) by Bob Wills Orchestra and 'Worried Mind' (Okeh) by Ted Daffan's Texans. Each is corny, but good." Left to right: Frankie Kinman, Jerry Elliott, Ted Daffan, Dickie Harrell, Johnny Strawn, Jimmy Brown. Courtesy of Kevin Coffey.

The Jerry Elliott Band. "Jerry's at the mic with the standard guitar," informed Kevin Coffey. "As the drumhead said, the drummer is Bop Johnson. The fiddler is Charlie Mitchell (can't tell it here, but he was missing an ear), and the steel player is Veda Mae Spoon." Veda Mae also appears in these pages with the Paradise Ramblers and the Texas Cowgirls, as Marge and Margie. A 1941 *Radio Varieties* article said that Veda Mae was "the live wire" of the Texas Cowgirls. Courtesy of Kevin Coffey.

Pioneers

Country-western journalist Floy Case of Fort Worth may not have seen herself as a pioneer, but she was. The Country Music Foundation in Nashville officially said so in 1984. She began writing about hillbilly and cowboy performers in the 1930s. Her popular column, Down Bluebonnet Way, was published in the nationally distributed *Mountain Broadcast and Prairie Recorder*, where she became an associate editor.

In a 1947 issue of the magazine, Floy reported, "The new HAL HORTON hillbilly audience participation show, CORNBREAD MATINEE, quickly outgrew the KRLD studios, and in order to accommodate the vast crowd that gathers to witness these informal and unpredictable broadcasts, [the show] moved over to the KESSLER THEATER in Oak Cliff. . . . The old maestro, BOB WILLS and his incomparable TEXAS PLAYBOYS played to a packed house here at the CASINO, one of the south's finest ballrooms. . . . Born in Hall County, Bob rode a box car into Ft. Worth, back in the '20s, and auditioned for his first radio job with a borrowed fiddle!"

Floy Case was the first to give Hank Thompson nationwide ink, and she became especially good friends with Ernest Tubb and with the Blue Yodeler's widow, Carrie Rodgers. The Texas Troubadour recorded a song that Floy cowrote, "I'm Beginning to Forget You," in 1945. "I'm especially proud of the recording we did," Tubb wrote in a letter to Floy and her husband J. C. Case. "I kinda think this number may go places." Closing the letter, ET said he was "all out of soap."

Another female songwriter in Cowtown, Diane Johnston, won first place in a 1950 songwriting contest sponsored by Elston Brooks's *Star-Telegram* column, "Just For Fun." She received a hundred bucks for her tune, "High in the Saddle and Lonesome for You" about "a cowhand who rode the range with only his shadow for company." Two years later, she dashed off "Can't Shake the Sands of Texas From My Shoes" in seven minutes, which Gene Autry soon crooned on the silver screen. She cowrote "Miles and Miles of Texas," popularized decades later by Asleep at the Wheel.

Mrs. Johnston also wrote some songs with her son Bob, who eventually rambled out of state to produce recordings by Johnny Cash, Leonard Cohen, Simon & Garfunkel, and Bob Dylan.

Bill Case and the Melody Boys were among the many string bands with daily shows on DFW radio, circa 1930s. Bill Case, fiddle, J. C. Case, mandolin, Homer Hargrove, guitar. The announcer was Mike Gallagher. Courtesy of Johnny Case.

Crazy

An hour west of Fort Worth, the town of Mineral Wells had a significant impact on the history of country-western music. While Crazy Water and Crazy Water Crystals, the resort city's chief exports, also sponsored big band broadcasts, the *Crazy Barn Dance* and other programs throughout Texas and the South and as far north as Canada presented such hillbilly and Western artists as Bill Monroe, Hank Snow, Bob Wills, Pee Wee King, Foy Willing, Wade and J. E. Mainer, the Crazy Blue Ridge Hillbillies, and the Crazy Tennessee Ramblers.

In 1934, when Nashville's *Grand Ole Opry* was divided into fifteen-minute segments that were sold to sponsors, the first company to purchase a slot was Crazy Water Crystals of Mineral Wells. And noted singer/songwriter Tom Russell was so inspired by the Crazy town that he wrote a song entitled "Mineral Wells."

She told him of a fountain of youth,
in the hot Texas earth.
It'll heal you and renew you.
It's somewhere west of Fort Worth.
Mineral Wells. . . .

Floy Case occasionally sat in with the Melody Boys on accordion. Courtesy of Johnny Case.

Record release party for Hank Thompson's "Humpty Dumpty Heart" in downtown Dallas, late 1940s. Metro Music, operated by Hugh Fowler, kneeling (with his arm draped on Billie Fowler's knee), and *Cornbread Matinee* deejay Hal Horton, far left, published the sheet music for the song. Hank is the tall drink of water holding a glass. Courtesy of Trinity River Music.

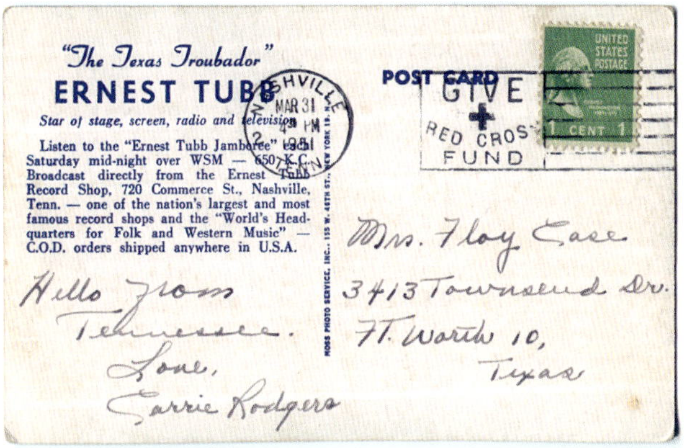

"The Texas Troubador"
ERNEST TUBB
Star of stage, screen, radio and television
Listen to the "Ernest Tubb Jamboree" each Saturday mid-night over WSM — 650 K.C. Broadcast directly from the Ernest Tubb Record Shop, 720 Commerce St., Nashville, Tenn. — one of the nation's largest and most famous record shops and the "World's Headquarters for Folk and Western Music" — C.O.D. orders shipped anywhere in U.S.A.
POST CARD
GIVE
RED CROSS
FUND
Mrs. Floy Case
3413 Townsend Dr.
Ft. Worth 10,
Texas
Hello from
Tennessee.
Love,
Carrie Rodgers

Floy Case became good friends with Jimmie Rodgers's widow, Carrie Rodgers, and ghosted many of Mrs. Rodgers's published writings. Courtesy of Johnny Case.

Cover of Hal Horton songbook published by Metro Music. Horton was a popular Dallas radio personality and host of the programs *Hillbilly Hit Parade* and *Cornbread Matinee*. Courtesy of Trinity River Music.

Universal Mills artists Jimmie and Leon Short were known on radio as "Smoky" and "Bashful" when they played with Ernest Tubb in San Angelo, prior to ET's Fort Worth days. Tubb biographer Ronnie Pugh credits Jimmie Short with playing a style of melody that "would set the standard for all of Tubb's subsequent guitarists." Courtesy of Johnny Case.

Hank Thompson had this outfit made to promote one of his earliest records, "Humpty Dumpty Heart." Courtesy of Steve Bonner.

No one could ever accuse the North Texas Devil's Box man, known as Fiddlin' Rook Kirk (a Kentucky native), of not bringing the energy. Shown here at—er, under—the microphone at Dallas's KRLD, where he was playing with Bill & Joe Callahan. Courtesy of Kevin Coffey.

Dallas-raised Cleo Raymond, wrote Jacquielynn Floyd in the *Dallas Morning News,* "was a hillbilly-band princess in the years when Western music ruled the airwaves and packed the clubs. She toured with the legendary Tex Ritter and with Gus Foster and the Texas Roundup. She shared the stage with Ernest Tubb and Bob Wills and Roy Acuff, and she had her own band, too: Miss Cleo and the Texas Farmhands." The Farmhands toured with LBJ's notorious 1948 Senate campaign, when Lyndon, stung by his 1941 Senate defeat at the hands of Pappy O'Daniel, realized it was a good idea to have a hillbilly band backing one up on the trail. When the reporter met Cleo, it was 2001 and the veteran accordionist was playing at a Rowlett church. "It was just a handful of ladies at a potluck lunch," Floyd wrote, "but Cleo could just as easily have been fronting for the Texas Farmhands at the *Big D Jamboree*. She gives every performance all she's got." Courtesy of Kevin Coffey.

J. B. Brinkley's long, busy career is emblematic of the many country-western and western swing musicians in DFW who multitasked into jazz, pop, rock, etc. In the late 1930s, Brinkley sang with the Crystal Springs Ramblers, then moved to the Light Crust Doughboys. In 1945 JBB and his Swingtime Band played the Hilarity Club on Roberts Cutoff at Jacksboro Highway. In '46 JBB "and his Doughboys" were at Club Morocco. Later that year, the band was called "his Great Orchestra." In '47 he sang with Dick Dickerson's Orchestra at the Skyliner. '49 saw him in on radio and TV on *Melody Shop* and in the Cedar Ridge Boys and the TV Trio with Lee and Dale Woodward, Jack Gipson, Cecil Brower, Carroll Hubbard, Bob Bohm, Claude Ware, Betty Brockwell, and Jimmy Lehmann. (That New Year's Eve his orchestra played a sweet gig on the Baker Hotel roof in Mineral Wells.) In '50 he played guitar in The Country Cousins square dance band with Dixie Harper, Gipson, and Pitts on WBAP-TV's *Crossroads Store.* Brinkley and Gipson also appeared on the show as a comedy team. '51 found him on WBAP's *Barn Dance* with Jack Valentine "and all the gang" and also on a Saturday morning kid's show as "Billy the Kid, Your Favorite Cowboy Star." The next year, JBB and the Westerners featured Gipson, Bohm, and Harold Tomlin, and also as a member of Bob Bohm's Band. In 1960, Brinkley descended into the notorious Cellar to play jazz guitar. In '64 his outfit was called the JBB Combo, and in 1970 JBB broke out his banjo to play a benefit for United Way with Red Woodward's seventeen-piece orchestra. Along the way, he found time to be a go-to session player for recordings produced by Major Bill Smith and Joe Leonard's Linn Records and Kliff Records, which earned JBB a bit of cult status as a rock 'n' roll guitarist among aficionados of rockabilly and early rock 'n' roll. Courtesy of the Portal to Texas History.

The wayward whims of showbiz are likely all that kept Charlie Mitchell (standing, second from right) and the Southern Stars from becoming hillbilly heroes. Mitchell's son Charlie kept the family's Fort Worth music tradition going into the twenty-first century. Courtesy of Charlie Mitchell.

Courtesy of Charlie Mitchell.

On the road, the five brothers from Paris, Texas, called themselves the Williams Boys, but when they were home, making music with their sisters, wives, and children, they were just known as the Williams Family. Courtesy of Wm Wms.

"YOUR CRAZY PROGRAMMERS IN ACTION." Left to right: Guy (Curly) Woodward, Dale (Pee Wee) Woodward, Johnny (Uncle Oscar) Jordan, Lorraine Miles the Yodeling Cowgirl (our child Sacred Harp singer from Chapter Five), Frank (Great Lover) McMordie, Maurice (Pinky) Pendery, and E. L. (Stinky) Davis. Announcer Conrad Brady had just stepped out for some Crazy Water. Courtesy of George Gimarc.

Lorraine Miles on tour with the Crazy Gang, 1939. Courtesy of Chloe Webb.

In "real life," Cousin Abner, a platter-spinning personality on Dallas's KSKY, was John Hitt. An artist himself, Hitt made one record for Dallas label Star-Talent and also managed Hank Thompson for a time. Courtesy of Kevin Coffey.

Photograph of WBAP Saturday Morning Roundup Gang, featuring members of The Red Hawks band. Standing left to right: Ray Berry, Red Woodward, Cecil Brower, Ted Gouldy, Jack Gipson, Kenneth Pitts, Andy Schroder. Seated left to right: Dale Woodward, Ted Graves, Dixie Harper, Billyevan Gober, Marvin Montgomery. Circa 1945. Courtesy of the Portal to Texas History.

George "Big Dean" Turner, with guitar, swapped a pocket watch for his first instrument. He became known as "The Red River Valley Boy" on Sherman radio before moving to Fort Worth, where his band, with "Little Dean," at left, Ray Yates, Charlie Owens, and Bill Hudson, was mostly active in the '40s. In Fort Worth he hosted the popular *Turner's Turntable* on KWBC and produced the *Cowtown Round-Up*, a live show mixing touring stars with local talent. "Little Dean," shown sitting on a porch after a performance for US Speaker of the House Sam Rayburn, became a Fort Worth guitar ace, as witnessed in the image with an early Les Paul. (Note: Re. Dean's handwritten caption, the first Gibson Les Paul was not produced until 1952.) Even after his star had dimmed, Big Dean continued for the love of music, sharing his traditional country-western sound in churches and nursing homes. Courtesy of Kevin Coffey and Record Town.

Courtesy of Competition Music, Fort Worth.

Al Dexter visits Big and Little Dean on the radio, circa 1943. Courtesy of Competition Music, Fort Worth.

Courtesy of Record Town, Fort Worth.

Either the Juvenile Baby's vocals are putting the steel-player to sleep, or he's just having a rough night! Doug Bragg can be seen over her shoulder. Courtesy of George Gimarc.

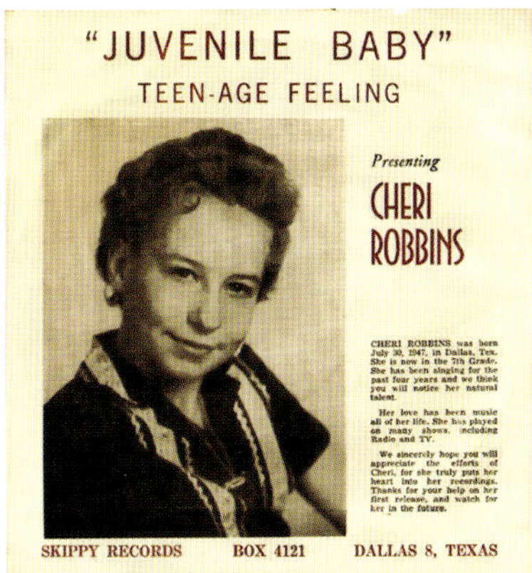

Born in Dallas in 1947, a young Cheri Robbins made appearances on the *Cowtown Jamboree* at Fort Worth's Majestic Theater. Images of her performances present a vernacular country-western style, but her recordings on Skippy Records and other labels seem to indicate a genre-straddler similar to early Brenda Lee. Courtesy of George Gimarc.

Courtesy of George Gimarc.

Dallas native Phil York began his audio engineering career with radio station KXOL's Sound City studio in 1965. He later worked with Marvin Montgomery at Sumet Sound before operating Autumn Sound in Garland and Big Y Productions and Yorktown Digital Works, both in Irving. Though he won three Grammy awards, recorded such major artists as Willie Nelson, the Rolling Stones, Jerry Jeff Walker, Ann-Margret, Trini Lopez, and Helen Reddy, and recorded the music for the c&w film *Tender Mercies,* he was also passionate about encouraging local, unknown artists. In 1979, he helped Dallas realtor Peggy Reeves with her album, *Shake You Loose.* Two years later, he recorded mariachi singer (and recent TCU PhD in English literature) Juan Hernandez at Joe T. Garcia's in Fort Worth. In 1992, he produced the music of Grand Prairie police officer Sgt. Martha DeWolfe. "He's the godfather and dean of Dallas and Texas recording arts," said Mesquite musician Art Greenhaw when York died at age seventy in 2012. "Phil turned down offers to leave Dallas...he just wanted to stay here and do everything he could to pump this area up." Another artist ventured, "He's probably up in heaven telling Stevie Ray Vaughan and Jimi Hendrix, 'I can make you sound better.'" Courtesy of George Gimarc.

CHAPTER NINE

Recording

From the Cornfield Symphony Orchestra to the Red Headed Stranger: Studio Recordings in Dallas-Fort Worth

"For the first time in history," announced the *Dallas Morning News* in November 1924, "phonograph records for nationwide distribution are to be made in Dallas by local artists." The General Phonograph Corporation recorded such Dallas ensembles as the Chenoweth Cornfield Symphony Orchestra and the Jack Gardner Orchestra on portable recording equipment, set up at 1917 Main Street, for release on its OKeh label. The sessions were arranged by Will J. Schnelle, manager of Texas Radio Sales, OKeh's area distributor.

OKeh representatives returned in October 1925 for another week of recording. Schnelle told the press at that time that, aside from the previous year's Dallas sessions, "no other recording has ever been done in Texas." The 1925 sessions included the Cornfield Symphony and the Gardner Orchestra, as well as the Bel Canto Quartet, Edgar Norris, Irene Taylor, Jimmie's Joys, College Ramblers, Jimmie Wilson's Catfish String Band, Doc and Mac, and McBeth, "the king of the harmonica."

As the twenties roared on, artists recording in Dallas-Fort Worth included the unique gospel figures Washington Phillips and Blind Willie Johnson. Jimmie Rodgers recorded in Dallas twice in 1929 and once in 1932. The last session, which took place at the Jefferson Hotel, included Dallas guitarist Bill Boyd playing on such tracks as "Hobo's Meditation."

When teen rock 'n' rollers in the Dallas suburbs began discovering classic American blues tunes on recordings by "British Invasion" bands in the 1960s, little did they know that some of those groundbreaking songs were first recorded thirty years earlier in a downtown Dallas studio at 508 Park. Built in 1930 and surviving today as Dallas's prime extant example of Zigzag Moderne architectural style, the structure was known as the Warner Brothers Building, from which films and soundtracks were distributed.

Brunswick Records was located on the third floor, where producer Don Law, an Englishman by birth, who had started with Brunswick as a bookkeeper, installed a recording studio in the late 1930s. Artists recording in the Depression-era studio included the Light Crust Doughboys, Bob Wills and his Texas Playboys, the Chuck Wagon Gang, the Stamps Quartet, W. Lee O'Daniel and his Hillbilly Boys, and many more. In 1939, the last year recordings were made at 508 Park, a number of Mexican American artists recorded there, including Gaytan y Cantu,

Paul and Paula were among the major's hitmakers. Originally turned down by several record labels, Paul and Paula inspired the creation of other duos, often on the same labels that rejected them. Courtesy of Phil York / George Gimarc.

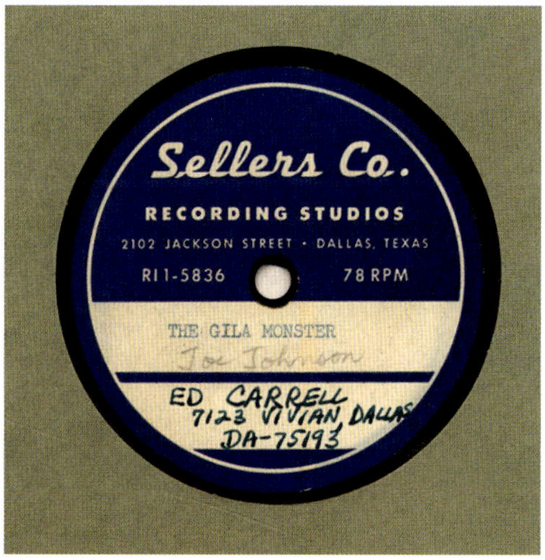

James Earl "Pop" Sellers opened what was possibly the first independent recording studio in the Southwest, Sellers Studio, in Dallas in 1936. He'd grown up on a farm near Midlothian and earned a physics degree from UT Austin. Experimenting with electronics, he converted a phonograph into a sound recording device. In 1937, Sellers obtained a Universal portable recording machine, and he was reportedly the first in the area to own an Ampex tape recorder, a condenser microphone, and a high-speed tape duplicator. In time, the artists recording at Sellers, many of whom called him "Pop" for his kind, grandfatherly manner, included the Levee Singers, the Novas, gospel pianist Marion Snider, Gene Summers, Gene Vincent, Stamps Quartet, the Light Crust Doughboys, Hank Thompson, Trini Lopez, and many others. Many a commercial message was recorded at Sellers as Dallas became known as the "Jingle Capitol of the World." Though it was not included in the 1959 anti-classic horror flick, *The Giant Gila Monster*, filmed near Dallas by colorful Big D radio innovator Gordon McLendon, Joe Johnson recorded "The Gila Monster" that same year at Sellers (acetate label shown here). Ed Carrell, the song's author and a Dallas salesman for General Foods, had approached popular bandleader (and tenor sax, vibes, and piano man) Joe Johnson at Jack Ruby's Vegas Club in the Oak Lawn area, where Johnson's combo had become a fixture, about recording the tune. A friend of Carrell's provided an introduction to Fess Parker, Disney's Davy Crockett, who had just started the Cascade record label and, according to local press reports, the tune "climbed into the Top Ten circle here last week." Courtesy of George Gimarc.

Fort Worth record empresario Major Bill Smith knew a "cotton pickin' hit!" when he saw one. Courtesy of Trinity River Music.

new systems himself," his widow Elizabeth told Wolfe.

Jim Beck died at age thirty-nine in May 1956. He had been cleaning recording heads with carbon tetrachloride without proper ventilation, and the poison lodged in his liver. At the time, Don Law had been planning to move all of Columbia's country-western recording from Los Angeles and Nashville to Beck's Dallas studio. And Decca had decided to follow suit.

"After Jim died," added Elizabeth Beck, "I like to never have sold his stuff, because nobody knew what it was; he had built it all himself, and nobody knew how to run it."

One of the most eccentric record producers in metro music history, Major Bill Smith, spawned a handful of hits in the 1960s. "Smith," wrote Martin Kohout in *The Handbook of Texas Music*, in a kind stroke of apparent understatement, "was a relentless self-promoter who seemed disinclined to let the facts get in the way of a good story, making the accounts of his life he told to various interviewers of somewhat dubious veracity. His bombastic manner earned him a reputation as a con man and hustler, but his savvy marketing instincts also made him a notable force in the recording industry."

Marvin "Smokey" Montgomery was partly responsible for one of the major's hits. In 1961 the

Light Crust Doughboys banjoist brought a young singer from Grapevine named Bruce Channel to Smith's studio in the basement of Fort Worth radio station KFJZ, where the major paid Delbert McClinton's band the Strait-Jackets five dollars a session as house musicians. Soon the tape machine was rolling with Delbert's harmonica intro to Channel's "Hey Baby!" and that spring the tune was #1 on the *Billboard* charts for three weeks.

A subsequent tour in 1962 took Smith, Montgomery, McClinton, and Channel to England, where a young group called the Beatles opened for the "Hey Baby!" hitmaker when Channel played Liverpool. And thus began the legend of Delbert teaching John Lennon the secrets of harmonica soul. McClinton downplays the story, but it sounds entirely logical.

In 1975, when Willie Nelson recorded his breakout album, *Red Headed Stranger*, his first for Columbia, he wanted to do it his way. On the advice of his harmonica player, Mickey Raphael, he chose to work at Autumn Sound Studios in Garland, Texas, with engineer Phil York. "I had known Phil for several years," Raphael told *Acoustic Magazine*, published in England. A Dallas community college student at the time, Raphael hung out at the studio after school and played anytime a project needed harmonica.

The album was the first time that Willie had recorded with his touring Family band. "The reason the album is so sparse is mainly because we were a small band, and we were hearing everything for the first time, listening and reacting," Raphael explained. "He was pretty much playing them stream-of-consciousness, and we played the songs a couple of times at the most. . . . There is just simplicity and so much silence on that record because we were all enamored of Willie and of how beautiful and simple the project was."

Too much simplicity, in the minds of the record company execs. They said it sounded like it'd been recorded in someone's living room and wanted to add strings and back-up vocals. But having been given creative control in his contract, Nelson insisted it be released as is. One exec who fell in love with the record relented and added his voice in favor of releasing the record. "It won't sell," he argued, "but it's special."

Welcomed by music fans as a work of rare authenticity, the album went platinum.

By 1985, Phil York (right) had reportedly "recorded more actual *Billboard* chart records than all other Dallas-Fort Worth area recording engineers combined." Courtesy of Phil York / George Gimarc.

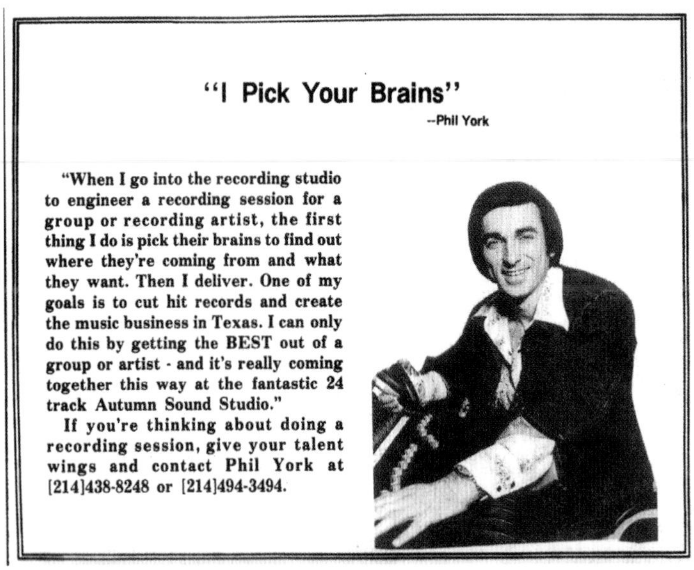

Courtesy of Phil York.

Born in Monclova, Coahuila, in 1917, Joe Azcona (at right) came to Texas with his family at age four. A jeweler by trade, his "Latin big band" was popular in the '40s and '50s. He also led a mariachi band.
Courtesy of DMAHL.

CHAPTER TEN

Tejano and Tex-Mex

¡Metro Musica!

Histories of Tejano and Tex-Mex music usually focus on musicians based in San Antonio, the Rio Grande Valley, and other communities closer to the Mexican border. But as Carlos E. Cuéllar noted in his 2004 book, *Stories from the Barrio: A History of Mexican Fort Worth*, "Wherever people go, their music always goes with them. Fort Worth's barrios swelled with music from the diverse regions of Mexico and Texas. Rancheras, polkas, mariachi, boleros, danzones, cumbias, and Tejano all found their way into the homes, dance halls, and ballrooms of Cowtown."

¡Musica! Our Rhythm, Our Heart, Our Soul, a 2017 exhibition produced by the Dallas Mexican American Historical League at the city's Latino Cultural Center, revealed an equally rich legacy in Big D. A "soundtrack to the Mexican American experience in Dallas," the show not only honored traditions that are *puro Mexicano*, but it also explored a musical community in conversation with other cultures, telling the stories of artists who were often multicultural before multiculturalism was cool.

When Joe Azcona, Henry Munoz, Abundio Ortiz, Freddie Cisneros, and other North Texas bandleaders and musicians gathered for a tribute concert to nonagenarian violinist Alfredo Casares at Dallas's Cruz Ballroom in 1991, publicity described Casares as "one of the first mariachi band leaders in Dallas." The earliest Alfredo Casares reference located is from 1929, when the musician directed the Mexican Serenaders group on Dallas radio station WFAA. One program announcement described the Serenaders as "a group of talented native Mexicans, who were at one time the official orchestral entertainers for Pancho Villa. . . . They feature folksongs of their country and play them as only real Mexicans can."

Two years later, as western swing swept through the metroplex in the 1930s, Casares—described by one critic as a "'hot' Mexican fiddler"—joined the Wanderers on WRR, led by Roy Newman. He went on to stroke the Devil's Box for a string of mostly Anglo outfits, including the Bird Branders, the Light Crust Doughboys, the Crazy Gang (sponsored by Crazy Water Crystals), and Jim Boyd's Men of the West. He also spent a mysterious spell playing with the Swift Jewel Cowboys in Memphis, Tennessee, reportedly under the pseudonym Jose Cortes.

Despite responding to multicultural influences, Casares never abandoned the traditions of his heritage. In 1948, for instance, Texas papers from Rockdale to Electra carried ads for a State Fair performance billed as a "fiesta of fun." Sponsored by Lone Star Gas, the "gorgeous setting inspired by colorful, romantic Modern Mexico" featured music by Alfredo Casares "and his six gay caballeros" with "exotic vocalist" Carmen Cervantes. A year later, his large ensemble, Professor Casares and His Boys, played the Cinco de Mayo celebration at Dallas's Pike Park. And in the 1950s, Casares served as emcee of the WFAA-TV program *Mexican Jamboree*, with the Fred Casares Orchestra backing guest performers.

The artistic direction of another Dallasite, Casares's nephew Alfonso Wesar, to whom Uncle Alfredo was an inspiration, further demonstrates the genre-spanning of North Texas's Hispanic

Pablo Alonzo and family, somewhere in Dallas's Little Mexico. Courtesy of DMAHL.

Clara Torres began her musical career in Dallas as a young girl. Courtesy of DMAHL.

The Royal Knights! Courtesy of DMAHL.

In March 1958, Juvey Gomez was fifteen years old and playing with Dallas rockabilly star Johnny Carroll. With permission from his mother and his teachers, he went on tour with Gene Vincent for a few weeks and appeared in the film, *Hot Rod Gang*. He also recorded with Vincent at Capitol Records in Los Angeles. They were in "Frank Sinatra's studio," and Juvey had the thrill of seeing jazz legend George Shearing at work. "I was already into jazz," Gomez told Robert Wilonsky in the *Dallas Observer* in 1998. "That was cooler than playing with Gene Vincent. And Gene knew it." Courtesy of DMAHL.

Born in Dallas's Little Mexico in 1938, Henry Munoz began playing professionally at age sixteen. "I was working as a bus boy at El Fenix. They had a little trio, and one night the piano player didn't show up. A co-worker said, 'This guy plays.' I said, 'No, I don't.' 'Yes, you do.' So I auditioned and got the job." Shown here leaning on the marimbas in 1975, Munoz was still playing in Dallas restaurants at age eighty in 2019. Courtesy of DMAHL.

Frank Sandoval and the Sky Tones onstage at the Hi-Ho Ballroom in Grand Prairie. Courtesy of DMAHL.

Bobby Butler, "el Charro Negro," with Little Joe and the Latinaires, performs at the Hi-Ho Ballroom. Courtesy of DMAHL.

A native of Brownsville, Juan "Johnny" Moa was inducted into the Tejano Roots Hall of Fame. He enjoyed performing at weddings, quinceañeras, and Dallas area night clubs that often featured Tejano music such as the Hi-Ho Ballroom. Moa was awarded two Purple Hearts and two Bronze Stars for his service in Vietnam. Seen here with his son Juanelo, Juan Moa passed away in 2019. Courtesy of DMAHL.

Conjunto Zarape recorded for Johnny Gonzales's Zarape Records. Courtesy of DMAHL.

The late great *conjunto* accordionist Angel Flores performs at Johnny Gonzales's El Zarape Ballroom in Dallas. Courtesy of DMAHL.

The True Kings Band! Courtesy of Crazy Chuy Hernandez.

The Sunlites onstage in Kaufman, Texas. "Crazy Chuy" Hernandez, with drumsticks, in recent years has broadcast an online Tejano music show from his home studio in Waxahachie. In 2003, Chuy was inducted in the Tejano R.O.O.T.S. Hall of Fame. Courtesy of Crazy Chuy Hernandez.

"If rock 'n' roll is your cup of tea," said the *Morning News* After Dark column in 1960, "Joe's gang will send you." Joe Ramirez's recordings on Dallas's Skippy label included the 1958 tune, "Mister Rock 'n' Roll." In 1960 his Jumping Jacks, representing Jimmy's Club on East Mockingbird, waged a "Battle of the Bands and Clubs" against Joe Johnson, representing Jack Ruby's Vegas Club, at the Hi-Ho Ballroom in Grand Prairie. Here, the Jumping Jacks pose with guitarist Bobby Rambo, recording star on Dallas's Abnak label. Courtesy of DMAHL.

Paul Guerrero Sr. was a Dallas big band musician. His son Paul Jr., seen here, was a renowned jazz drummer who performed with Stan Kenton before starting his own ensembles. Debra Smith, seen here on vocals, also came from a musical family. Her grandfather was big band leader Marcelino Marceleño. Courtesy of DMAHL.

Born in Dallas, Trini Lopez (left), seen here with Adolfo López Mateos, president of Mexico from 1958 to 1964, first recorded with the Big Beats in the late '50s before launching a wildly successful solo career. His chart hits included "Lemon Tree" and "If I Had a Hammer." Lopez also appeared in major feature films, and the two guitars he designed for Gibson in the 1960s are reportedly collectors' items. In 2002, he released the album *Legacy: My Texas Roots* with Art Greenhaw and brother Jesse Lopez. His appearance in Dallas was one of the highlights of DMAHL's 2017 exhibition on Dallas music. Lopez died of coronavirus at age eighty-three in 2020. Courtesy of DMAHL.

Sam the Sham and the Pharoahs hit the charts in the midsixties with "Wooly Bully" and "Little Red Ridin' Hood." Asked about the meaning of the term "sham," bandleader Sam Samudio said it was "rhythm-and-blues jargon for shuffling, twisting or jiving around to music." In 1982, Samudio contributed two Spanish-language songs to the Jack Nicholson film *The Border*. Courtesy of George Gimarc.

The frontman for Aztec Milk Temple, Scott Tucker, curated the DMAHL exhibition on Dallas music. Tucker's great-grandfather was Marcelino Marceleño. Courtesy of Scott Tucker.

Domingo "Sam" Samudio, born in Dallas, March 6, 1937. Courtesy of George Gimarc.

Johnny Carroll as he appeared on a lobby card for the
1957 Dallas-made film *Rock Baby, Rock It*.
Courtesy of David Dennard.

CHAPTER ELEVEN

Rockabilly, Rhythm and Blues, Early Rock 'n' Roll

Rhythm an Blue Music

Some Dallasites didn't appreciate Elvis Presley's frenetic choreography and lip-twitching vocals when he appeared in concert at the Cotton Bowl in 1956. His performance, sneered one resident in a letter to the *Dallas Morning News*, resembled "a shoat strangled on buttermilk in an ant bed."

Say *what*?

But seventeen-year-old Kay Wheeler of Dallas, founder of the world's first Elvis Fan Club, defended the ascending royalty of rock. "He just closes his eyes and starts singing and kind of hypnotizes us," she told the paper. "We can feel the music and pretty soon we start screaming and fainting. It's all a very natural reaction."

Indeed. An ecstatic response to the rhythmic wail that arose in the land in the 1950s was the most natural thing one could imagine. All across Dallas-Fort Worth performers and fans alike jumped and swooned to the avatars of rockabilly, rhythm and blues, and rock 'n' roll.

And while Mr. Presley's pelvis rent social norms asunder, artistic shifts in the North Texas music scene had been anticipating such cultural tremors for some time. As *Big D Jamboree* sensation Charline Arthur told writer Jay Brakefield, quoted in a Bear Family Records BDJ box set, "I was shakin' that thing onstage long before Elvis ever thought about it."

DFW music researcher Kevin Coffey noted in the same box set, "While white hillbilly musicians responding to blues or rhythm and blues was nothing new in 1953-4, there was something different, more deliberate and brash, about the way young bands like [Sid Erwin and the Western Melody Makers] were mixing the genres. In North Texas, they called it 'Cat Music.'"

Formed in Dallas in 1958, the Nightcaps had hits with "Wine, Wine, Wine" and "Thunderbird" on the local Vandan label. A Nightcaps platter was the first record Jimmie Vaughan ever bought with his own money, as he told *Dallas Morning News* scribbler Robert Wilonsky. "I learned how to play lead and rhythm and bass and drums off that record practically." Courtesy of George Gimarc.

In that delightful, wacky way that Europe's Texas-music-fans-on-steroids have of imagining the state's impossible geography, one blogger

Seen here with his early band the Royal Jokers, Fort Worth's Charlie Carey, second from left, went on to play lead guitar with Gary Lewis and the Playboys. He also performed with Chuck Berry, Conway Twitty, and Fats Domino. In 2016, he played a show in Euless with the town's singer-songwriter/chief of police Mike Brown. Courtesy of Charlie Carey / Record Town.

Dallas agent Tony Papa called the Big Beats, seen here in an early shot with Donny McCord, "the greatest group of its kind to come along since Freddy Bell and the Bellboys." Fronted at first by Trini Lopez, the band enjoyed a long run with many different members. In the 2010s, annual reunion shows snapped a lot of dormant synapses for longtime fans. Left to right: Donny McCord (whose father owned Dallas's McCord's Music store), Larry Randall, Jerry Zapata, Earl Slocumb, C.W. Kendall. Courtesy of David Dennard.

A young Gene Summers.
Courtesy of George Gimarc.

proclaimed, "In 1953-54 what is now called 'Cat music' was developed in the West Texas, more precisely in the Dallas area." (We can hear Amon Carter hollering right now.) The Canadian rockabilly author Craig Morrison anointed Dallas's Lew Williams "the Daddy of Texas Cat Music" for his tunes like "Cat Talk," first demo'd in 1954. Williams explained to Sheree Homer, in her 2015 book, *Catch that Rockabilly Fever*, that he was playing what became cat music before he first heard the term from Dallas studio engineer Jim Beck in 1953.

In the *All Music Guide*, Greg Adams defined cat music as "a musical form preceding the rock & roll era that combined souped-up hillbilly sounds with hep slang in what was essentially a hillbilly adaptation of R&B." Bill Mack, perhaps best-known in his later incarnation as the Midnight Trucker on WBAP (and not to be confused with the bassist Bill Mack, who played with Gene Vincent and other rockabillies), contributed 1956's "Cat Just Got Back in Town" during his own brief tour of duty as a rockin' billy.

"These are all high-school boys from down in Denton, Texas," said Red Foley, introducing Sid King and the Five Strings—formerly Sid Erwin and the Western Melody makers—on the *Ozark Jubilee* in 1955, as the Strings kicked off their bouncy tune, "Sag, Drag, and Fall." In a 2017 *D Magazine* article, Sid Erwin/King told writer Alex Macon that the Five Strings' sound was "hillbilly bebop." Eventually, the group dropped the flashy cowpoke couture in favor of a hepcat look. "I think we were too country for rock and too rock for country," Erwin reflected, identifying a trait shared by many Texas artists.

Charline Arthur might have simply been too supercharged with raw energy for a mainstream

Denton homeboys Sid King and the Five Strings, on the road at Lubbock's Cotton Club. Left to right: Billy Erwin, Dave White, Mel Robinson, Sid Erwin (King). Courtesy of Steve Bonner.

Sid King and the Five Strings before they dropped the Western duds in favor of a hepcat look. Left to right: Billy Erwin, Kenny Massey, Sid Erwin (King), Dave White, Mel Robinson. Courtesy of Steve Bonner.

Young Ronnie Dawson,
the Blonde Bomber!
Courtesy of George Gimarc.

The "female Elvis," Charline Arthur rocks the joint in Tyler, circa 1954. Buddy Brady on fiddle. Courtesy of David Dennard.

1950s audience to handle in a female performer. Born in a boxcar in Henrietta, Texas, in 1929, she grew up in a family of twelve children and plenty of musical excitation. Her parents were Pentacostal gospel performers, albeit apparently open-minded ones. Her father signed a document allowing her to travel and perform with a medicine show at age fifteen. Charline had first shown musical talent at age five, playing a homemade cigar-box guitar. Two years later, she got her first store-bought instrument with money saved from picking up roadside pop bottles.

Onstage in her prime, she was a wild woman, jumping off amplifiers, flailing on the floor while wailing away. Historians say she was the first female country singer to perform wearing pants. Some add that Elvis told her she was his mother's favorite singer. The Rockabilly Hall of Fame calls her "that kitty who wanted to be an original." Her first record, cut at Jim Beck's studio in 1949, was a song she wrote at age twelve, "I've Got the Boogie Blues."

A regular on the *Big D Jamboree* for several years, Arthur, like so many talented performers, never reached the major success many felt she deserved. "I was considered an outlaw," she said in 1986, a year before she died. "They couldn't mold me into a little cotton dress, but I worked harder than Elvis ever thought about."

While some regarded Charline Arthur as the female Elvis, another popular *Jamboree* artist, Johnny Carroll, was often seen as "Decca's answer to RCA's Elvis." Carroll's performances in the 1957 film *Rock Baby, Rock It*, shot in Dallas (and posted to YouTube), support British music writer Bill Millar's description of Carroll as the embodiment of the "full-throttle brand of snarl-faced rockabilly, a trifle wilder than the rest." Carroll was at his best, Millar wrote, "when he personified rockabilly's potent image: the sexy, half-crazed fool flailing away at a guitar and hollering his guts out."

Born in Cleburne to a fiddle-playing mother in 1937, Carroll purchased his first guitar with money earned at his job as a water boy in a POW camp during World War II. In the late '50s he became music director for the Cellar nightclubs in Dallas and Fort Worth.

Another Dallas area rockabilly artist, Ronnie Dawson, a.k.a. "the Blond Bomber," also grew up in a musical family. His father, Pinkie Dawson, led a western swing band called the Manhattan Merrymakers, and his mother Gladys led the choir at the Assembly of God church the family

Ronnie Dawson is the biggest cult hero of all—and he deserves to be." A rockabilly revival had begun in the '70s, picked up steam in the '80s, continued into the 1990s, and hasn't stopped yet, particularly in Europe. Reissues of rockabilly classics created a new generation of fans, and Dawson, Johnny Carroll, and Sid and Billy Erwin found themselves touring the continent.

Rockabilly fans both young and old occasionally drill down into the rumor that Ronnie Dawson and the black rockabilly star Ray Sharpe of Fort Worth once had plans to start a duo called Oreo Cookies. Some call Sharpe a rockabilly artist, others say he is R & B. Still others split the difference and call his music rock 'n' roll.

Growing up in Fort Worth's Public Housing Projects, Sharpe was nicknamed "the hillbilly" by neighbors for his love of country-western. "Country music was simple to follow, and it was simple for me to sing," he told John Makeig for a 1981 *Star-Telegram* piece. "I was learning it right off the radio. Yodeling, too." That same year, 1981, a Sharpe performance at Fort Worth's Sundancer Lounge was advertised as "The Boogie Blues and Funky Country Music."

Fort Worth's Fabulous Ray Sharpe, whose sound was once advertised as "The Boogie Blues and Funky Country Music." Courtesy of Record Town.

While incorporating so-called white idioms into his music, Ray Sharpe appealed to a mixed-race audience. At a 1959 gig at a black Fort Worth club named Watkins' Paradise, dozens of white and black patrons were arrested for "race mixing" on the dance floor, though charges were soon dropped. That same year, Sharpe was permanently installed on the American musical map with his hit song, "Linda Lu." Before long, he was appearing on *American Bandstand.*

Another Dallas soul singer who started out in the late 1950s, Bobby Patterson, shared formative influences with Ray Sharpe. "Every Saturday," Patterson told music writer Michael Corcoran in 2013, "I'd watch those country music TV shows. I'd see Buck Owens and Porter Wagoner and Ernest Tubb and they'd be telling stories with their songs. That's what I wanted to do." In fact, Patterson's first single was Tubb's seminal, Fort Worth-composed "Walkin' the Floor Over You." The Dallas soul singer released it in 1963, the same year the Warren Commission grilled him about Jack Ruby after learning that he had been playing at Ruby's Vegas Club and found his name in Ruby's apartment.

Performing into his mid-70s after a long career as a recording artist, producer, deejay, and record promoter, Patterson has been described as "a soul-singing legend." Like many Texas artists who might seem underappreciated at home, the singer reportedly gets a much bigger response in Europe.

Also in Dallas, another Ray was cooking up rhythms for his own blues. Ray Charles lived in Big D from around 1955 to 1958. Charles's biographer David Ritz (a slightly older graduate of the authors' Dallas high school) wrote that the artist's time in Dallas "was seminal to his early career. It was there where he cultivated many of the musicians and much of the music that would shape his career."

As Robert Wilonsky noted in a 2018 *Dallas Morning News* report on the house at the corner of Eugene and Myrtle Streets, one of those musicians was tenor sax player David "Fathead" Newman, a graduate of Dallas's Lincoln High. "I knew the town and dug it," Charles himself said of Big D. "Because Dallas didn't have the hurry-up stress of New York or L.A., I could kick back and figure out what I wanted to play and how I wanted to play it."

One of the most soulful artists to ever call Dallas home, Bobby Patterson has enjoyed a long career that continued in 2020. Courtesy of George Gimarc.

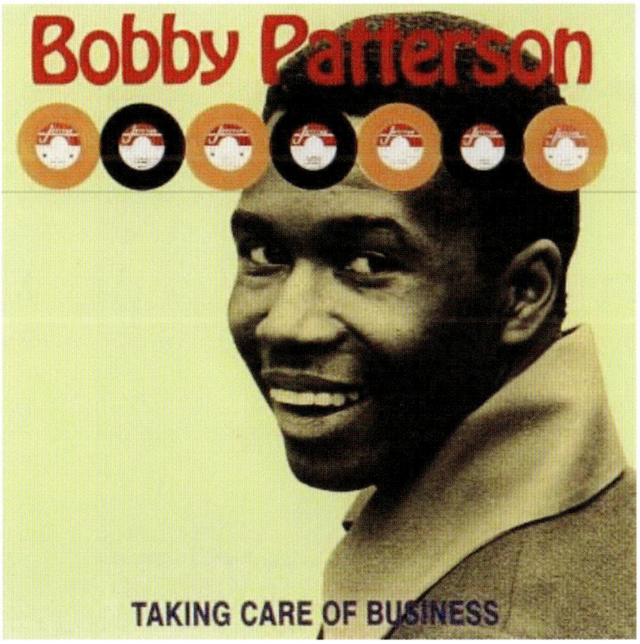

Courtesy of Ace Records Ltd.

Tenor sax man and bandleader Big Bo Thomas brought such artists as James Brown and Gladys Knight to perform at his Dallas clubs, the Empire Room, the Peacock Bar, and Zanzibar (not to be confused with the Fort Worth Zanzibar). He also owned his own label, Gay Shel Records, named for his daughter Gayle and his son Sheldon. Courtesy of Gayle Thomas.

"Big Bo Show, The Greatest Show on Earth" included R. L. Griffin, Dallas's "Right Reverend of the Blues," a.k.a. "Ting-a-Ling," who fronted Big Bo's band The Arrows for eight years at the Empire Room (later known as the Ascot Room) at 1710 Hall Street. Originally from Kilgore, Griffin later owned the Dallas clubs Blues Alley and R. L.'s Blues Palace #2. Courtesy of Sumter Bruton / Record Town.

After Big Bo's big band success, and before he formed the Arrows, he pared down the group to six satisfied musicians, and enjoyed immense notoriety in the Dallas R & B clubs of the day. Courtesy of Gayle Thomas.

Among the Big D venues Charles played was the American Woodman Hall on Oakland Avenue and the Empire Ballroom on Hall Street. The latter was owned by tenor sax player and bandleader William "Big Bo" Thomas. Born in Forney to a sharecropper family that moved into Dallas when he was twelve, Big Bo started his musical career with a seventeen-piece dance orchestra after serving in the army during World War II.

The big band was soon retooled into a smaller outfit, Big Bo and his Satisfied Six, and then Big Bo and his Arrows. Thomas eventually owned his own record label, in addition to at least two other nightspots, but in 1962 he released "Big Bo's Twist" on Dallas's Duchess label. The "raucous disc" reportedly sold some 76,000 copies in two days.

That same year, over in Cowtown, Delbert McClinton, one of the most soulful voices to ever emerge from North Texas, was recording with one of his early bands, the Strait-Jackets. He'd experienced the power of music while visiting family in Sweetwater at age twelve in 1952. As he recounted to Diana Finlay Hendricks in her 2017 biography, *Delbert McClinton: One of the Fortunate Few*, his Uncle Earl of Sweetwater was a mean and unpredictable drunk. And when Earl heard a Carl Smith tune being sung in his backyard and demanded to know who it was, Delbert figured he was in for it.

The boy fessed up, and Uncle Earl "went nuts" with praise, calling Aunt Marie out and making Delbert sing it again. For the rest of the visit, Earl would take Delbert to the donut shop at 5:30 a.m. before heading to work at Vandervoort Milk and make him sing Lefty and Hank for the locals. "I was the biggest attraction in Sweetwater before 6 a.m.," McClinton recalled. Music softened mean-assed Uncle Earl.

Delbert's life changed forever in the summer of 1954, before he turned fifteen. Hearing "Honey Hush" by Big Joe Turner blasting across a field from speakers at a drive-in restaurant, he stood still, taking it in. "I felt something that started in my ears and ran through me like an electrical shock . . . that music. It touched my soul. Until that day, I didn't know music could do that to you."

In the '50s and early '60s, McClinton told Hendricks, there were two kinds of live music in Fort Worth, "real sawhorse" country and black music. In 1957 Delbert experienced his "first real live performance onstage" when he sang Ray Price's "Crazy Arms" at the Big V Jamboree near the Fort Worth area community of White Settlement. Before long, he was fronting white R & B groups and backing up touring black artists at the Top Hat, Red Devil Lounge, Crystal Springs, Covered Wagon Ballroom, and other venues.

By 1959, the Strait-Jackets had become the house band at Jack's Place on the Mansfield Highway, a strip almost as notorious as the Jacksboro Highway. Underage drinking was a specialty at Jack's, and a neon mule on the sign out front tipped patrons off. If the mule wasn't kicking, it meant there was gonna be a raid. Hearing Jimmy Reed's "Honest I Do" on KNOK while driving to Jack's one night, Delbert heard another sound that touched his soul, the harmonica. Blues harmonica soon became the perfect companion to his world-weary voice, rough, ragged, wise, and full of life. A voice like no other, chiseled and tuned in the juke joints of old Fort Worth.

*Dawson may have mixed up the chronology of these events. A 1936 *Dallas Morning News* article indicates that Pinkie's auto accident happened in that year. And Kevin Coffey confirms that Ronnie's father continued playing for some years after the accident before retiring prematurely.

The MelloTones were formed in '57, with Vonnie Lightfoot, Bob Cowan, Henry Brunner, and Clark Wilson. Upon hearing that there was another MelloTones, they changed the name to the Martells around 1960. They opened for Bo Diddley at Louann's in Dallas and backed up the Coasters at the Tracer Club. Courtesy of Phil York / George Gimarc.

The Strait-Jackets, with "Good Rockin' Ray" Torres on drums. Courtesy of Betty Torres.

JACK'S PLACE
OPEN EVERY NIGHT TO THE PUBLIC
3112 MANSFIELD HIWAY
THE STRAIT JACKETS
RHYTHM AN BLUE MUSIC
WED.—THUR.—FRI. AND SATURDAY NIGHTS
TONITE AND SATURDAY 60c PER PERSON
For Your New Year's Reservation Call JE 5-9305—$3 Per Couple
Sat. Jan. 2nd—Big Joe Turner and Jimmie Nelson in the Battle of the Blues

"RHYTHM AN BLUE MUSIC" by "THE STRAIT JACKETS." Courtesy of Ted Tucker.

The Strait-Jackets, 1957. Left to right: Billy Cox, sax; Ray Clark, drums; Delbert McClinton, vocals; Robert Harwell, guitar (Les Paul); Art Holland, guitar (Strat). Courtesy of James Pennebaker.

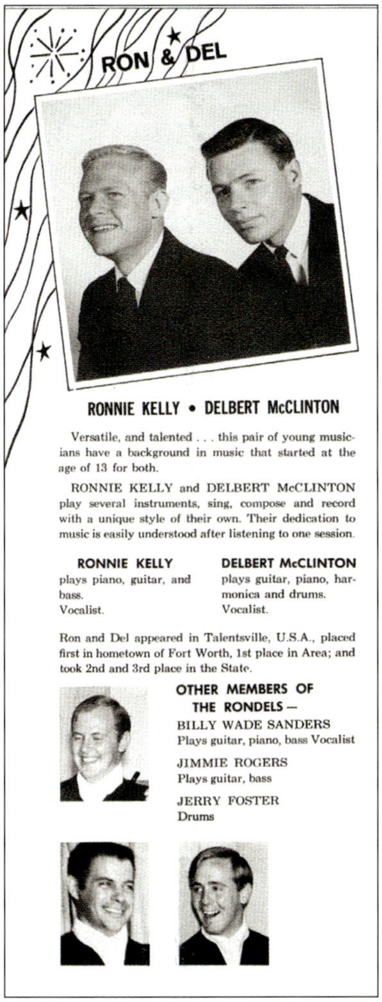

RONNIE KELLY • DELBERT McCLINTON

Versatile, and talented . . . this pair of young musicians have a background in music that started at the age of 13 for both.

RONNIE KELLY and DELBERT McCLINTON play several instruments, sing, compose and record with a unique style of their own. Their dedication to music is easily understood after listening to one session.

RONNIE KELLY
plays piano, guitar, and bass.
Vocalist.

DELBERT McCLINTON
plays guitar, piano, harmonica and drums.
Vocalist.

Ron and Del appeared in Talentsville, U.S.A., placed first in hometown of Fort Worth, 1st place in Area; and took 2nd and 3rd place in the State.

OTHER MEMBERS OF THE RONDELS —

BILLY WADE SANDERS
Plays guitar, piano, bass Vocalist

JIMMIE ROGERS
Plays guitar, bass

JERRY FOSTER
Drums

Another early Delbert group, the Rondels were named for their two lead vocalists. Courtesy of George Gimarc.

Delbert and the Rondels in Phil York's Studio. Courtesy of Phil York / George Gimarc.

Gene Summers and the Rebels were students at Arlington State College when they released their first record, "Straight Skirt," in 1958, which James McClung, left, wrote. Playing the Gretsch next to him is Glenn Keener, then Gene, with Charlie Mendias on drums, Mel Robinson on sax (who was in the Five Strings) and Dave Martin on bass, who was one of the founding members of Sam the Sham's Pharoahs. Courtesy of Phil York / George Gimarc.

Bobby Crown's dad played bass fiddle in a western swing band, Ernest Winnett and the Texas Trailblazers. After the band's singer got young Bobby interested in vocalizing, some of his early gigs were at the *Cowtown Hoedown* and the Lavida Club on the Mansfield Highway. Bobby said the Lavida was "pretty wild—folks were fightin' with tire tools and stuff in there." One critic pronounced Crown's recordings "Your Conscience" and "One Way Ticket" as "one of the most brilliant two-sided rockabilly classics of the ages." Courtesy of George Gimarc.

Joe Wilson and the Sabres at the Irving Theatre.
Courtesy of Trinity River Music.

Joe Wilson, at microphone, and the Sabres.
Courtesy of Trinity River Music.

Courtesy of George Gimarc.

Bruce Channel's 1961 recording, "Hey Baby!" cowritten with Margaret Cobb, was a "cotton pickin' smash!" on Major Bill's LeCam label before it went nationwide on Mercury. Featuring Delbert McClinton's distinctive harmonica intro, the hit song led to a tour of England, where a new group called the Beatles opened for the Fort Worth artists. Courtesy of Phil York / George Gimarc.

Jerry Fisher, who later became lead vocalist of Blood, Sweat, and Tears, formed the Night Beats in the mid-1960s. They played a regular Dallas circuit of clubs like The Losers, Gringo's, and Nero's Nook. In '64, the group featured Fisher on vocals and piano, Altice Moore on vibes and tenor, Dean McDaniels on trumpet and bass, drummer Jazzbo Jenzen, and Larry Pierce on organ and vibes. The *Dallas Morning News*'s Dallas After Dark column seemed fixated on the Beats' hairdos, commenting once on their "Beatle-type" styles and tight suits, another time noting that the group which once "boasted the longest hair in showbiz" now had crew cuts. Tony Zoppi wrote that "Fisher's hoarse vocals sound amazingly similar to Ray Charles." Courtesy of Trinity River Music.

Born James Mullins in 1941, the popular Dallas-based R & B rocker Jimmy Velvet—a.k.a. Jimmy Velvit—signed a record deal in 1961 with WRR's influential deejay Jim Lowe, who said Velvit sounded like a white Lonnie Johnson. Velvet/Velvit recorded over one hundred songs at Phil York's Dallas area studio. Courtesy of Sumter Bruton.

Little Johnny Shaw, at the Hi-Ho Ballroom, backed up by James Anderson and his band. "Little Johnny could do every move James Brown did," says Anderson. Courtesy of James Anderson.

FOR YOUR DANCING AND ENTERTAINMENT......SELECT ONE OF THESE BIG SPOTS

$1,000,000 ENTERTAINMENT CENTER

MAKE NEW YEAR'S EVE RESERVATION NOW

HiHo
2315 W. JEFFERSON
AN2-6446

NEW YEAR'S EVE FEATURING JOE WILSON with LITTLE JOHNNY SHAW and the HIHO SHABANG

RITZ
STARLITE ROOM
COUNT DIBRELL and the STARLIGHTERS
NEW YEAR'S EVE
2321 W. JEFFERSON
AN2-9378

HOLLYWOOD A-GO! GO!
2313 W. JEFFERSON
DANCE TO THE HOLLYS NEW YEAR'S EVE
OPEN TILL 2 AM

ADMISSION 67¢ TO EACH CLUB -- ASK FOR COMBINATION TICKET

Courtesy of James Anderson.

Buddy Miller was the emcee of a weekly show on Fort Worth's KTVT-TV called the *Hi Ho Shabang*, circa 1965-66. Regulars and guests on the program included Jimmy Velvit, Sonny Satin, Little Paul, The Panther A-Go-Go Girls, Joe Wilson, Little Johnny Shaw, and Gene Summers. Courtesy of James Anderson.

Bunched together on W. Jefferson in Grand Prairie, the Hi-Ho Ballroom, the Ritz Starlite, and the Hollywood A-Go-Go made a happening scene circa 1950s and '60s. Courtesy of DMAHL.

Popular soul artists Charles Gray and Les Watson with the Panthers onstage at Dallas's Blackout Club on Lovers Lane. Courtesy of George Gimarc.

Charles Gray, Les Watson, and the Panthers. "These guys put down a sound as fat as any I've heard in Big D," said Irving Harrigan of KLIF. "If you haven't heard them, you've missed one of the toughest combos around." Courtesy of George Gimarc.

Carter Buschardt, left, and Lou Bovis, center (son of Louann Bovis) with unknown musicians, playing at a South Dallas club. Courtesy of Carter Buschardt.

Courtesy of Ted Tucker.

According to popsike.com, an archive of past record auctions, Leslie Finney II, a.k.a. Finney Mo, Finnimo, and Finni-Moe, cut several singles that were all "in the same groove as Big Bo and the Arrows....fun R&B with a roadhouse feel." One was 1963's "Shake that Thing" on Fort Worth's JELLO-JIM Records. Another, "Finney Mo and His West Dallas Boys live at the River Club in Dallas," made Greil Marcus's "Real Life Rock Top Ten" list in *The Believer* of February 2014. Marcus writes, "[T]his underwater performance from 1976 is worlds away from any sort of conventional rock 'n' roll or R&B—it sounds like a secret tape Van Morrison kept as a magic lantern to rub when the spirit left him. The musicians slither along the riverbed; Finney rises every minute or so to call out what sounds like 'blind robber blind' over and over. You realize there's going to be no story....Does he really shout 'Stackerlee!' at the end?" By the early '80s, added popsike, the cool goofer had evolved a quasi-drag comedy act in which he sang R & B standards, which led to a $10,000 signing bonus with Malaco Records. "To celebrate his good fortune," reported popsike, "he and some of his South Dallas buddies proceeded to party down, and they ran through the $10,000.00 signing bonus by drinking a huge amount of cheap wine and beer for a solid month. At the end of that month, Finnimo had a heart attack and died." Courtesy of Ted Tucker.

Lil' Shylo and Good Time Charlie remain mysterious, but Paul English long kept the beat, whether bip-bop or not, for Willie Nelson. Courtesy of George Gimarc.

Courtesy of George Gimarc.

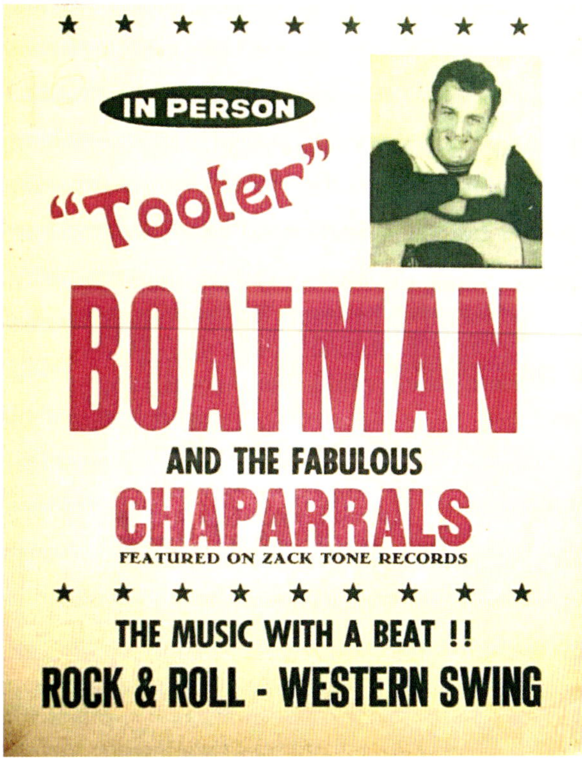

Born in Mineral Wells in 1936, Tooter Boatman was reportedly killed by a drunk driver in 1964. Many of Tooter's tunes were recorded at Danny Wolfe's studio in Stephenville and written by Wolfe. "Tooter was a great rockabilly singer," said Major Bill Smith. "He could make a guitar walk down the street. All Texan, he had a finger missing but could still play that guitar." British horse racing and rock 'n' roll blogger Simon Nott wrote that Tooter "and his band The Chaparrals released a rip roaring slab of scream laden, snare jangling, piano murdering, slap bass rockabilly in the shape of 'Thunder and Lightning' and 'The Will Of Love' which you really need to hear before you die." Courtesy of George Gimarc.

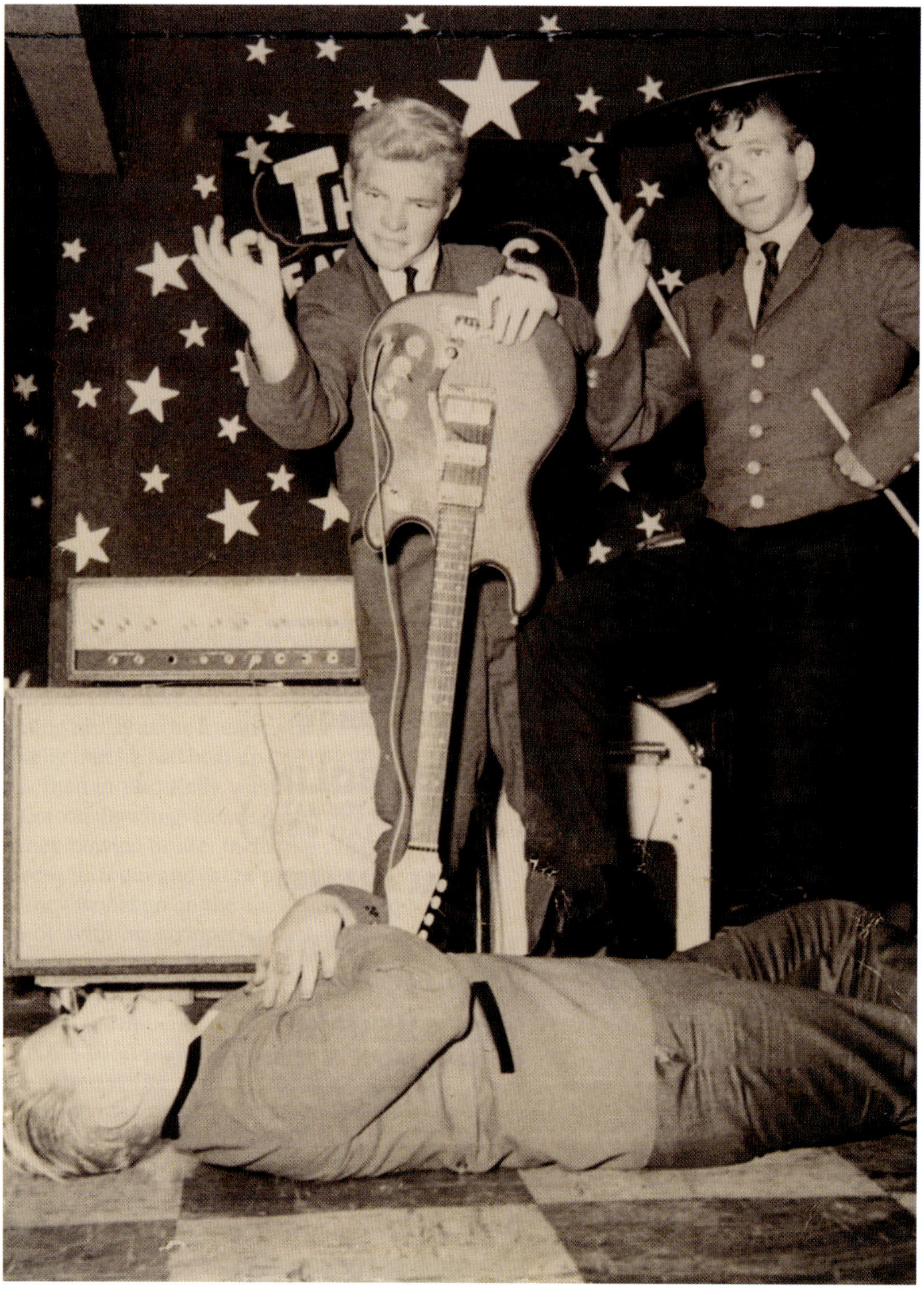

The American Blues (a.k.a. The Warlocks). Rocky Hill, guitar; Dusty Hill, bass; and Little Richard Harris, drums. In addition to the psychedelic blues of Rocky's lead guitar, they were known for Little Richard's hour-long drum solos on Sunday afternoons at Lee Park. This photo appears to show the band in their high school days, when they were known as The Starliners. Courtesy of Lady Kunkle.

CHAPTER THIRTEEN

Sixties Forever

Born to Be Wilde

"In the Sixties, people wanted everything to be wild," says Vicky Williams. "That's partly why my mother went by the stage name of Lady Wilde. It was also inspired by Oscar Wilde's mother." Lady Jane Wilde, who wrote poetry under the pen name Speranza, probably would have been right at home in the 1960s. A fiery campaigner for women's rights and other causes, she also loved to shock Victorian sensibilities with her outrageous costumes. In Dublin and London, her literary salons drew such luminaries as William Butler Yeats.

The singer Lady Wilde, whose real name was Mary Smith, sometimes cited as Marie Smith, represents the most tangible evidence of the 1960s "British Invasion" in Dallas-Fort Worth. Though North Texas guitarists would sometimes find themselves repressing their twangs to elocute with bloody English accents, or doing the Pete Townshend windmill, Lady Wilde is the only known British musician who actually physically invaded and set up shop in Dallas and Tarrant counties. "She was a Liverpool gal who had performed at the Cavern Club," adds Vicky. "She came to the states nineteen and pregnant, married to an American soldier from Dallas."

The only known British "invader" who showed up in Dallas-Fort Worth during the sixties and stayed, Mary (or Marie) Smith performed as Lady Wilde. Courtesy of James Anderson.

By 1965 she was the lead singer with Lady Wilde and the Warlocks, performing at Louann's in Dallas and Panther Hall in Fort Worth, where the marquee chopped the "e" off her name. (I guess Panther Hall ain't heared of Oscar Wilde.) One of the Warlocks, the future ZZ Top bassist Dusty Hill, says in the documentary film, *ZZ Top: That Little Ol' Band from Texas*, "In 1964, in Dallas, if you had someone from England in your band, that was it. You got bookings."

After leaving the Warlocks, Lady Wilde recorded dozens of songs with a band called Rolls Royce and the Wheels, one of which, "Poor Kid," became a regional hit. Wheels member James Anderson recalls that record promoters thought she sounded too much like Dusty Springfield. Mary Smith became a nurse, raised a family in Waxahachie and Ennis, and occasionally sang

Panther Hall left off that all-important e.
Courtesy of Andellyn Purvis-Hungerford.

Liverpool's Lady Wilde For Palace

Lady Wilde and the Warlocks, a modern music group fronted by one of the newest distaff singers from Liverpool, England, will make a special lobby appearance at 7:15 p.m. Friday at the Palace Theater.

The performance will be in conjunction with the new British-made musical, "Ferry Cross the Mersey." The film, starring Gerry and the Pacemakers, opened Thursday.

Lady Wilde and the Warlocks will present a short concert and Miss Wilde will answer questions from the audience about her native city, Liverpool, which has produced so many of the recording world's newest rages.

Lady Wilde, before coming to American, worked in many of the cellar clubs in Liverpool made famous by The Beatles, Gerry and the Pacemakers and other singers and instrumentalists.

Lady Wilde and the Warlocks just completed a month-long engagement at Dallas' original discotheque, Disc a Go Go.

LADY WILDE
. . . With the Warlocks

From Don Safran's *Dallas Morning News* column.
Courtesy of Vicky Williams.

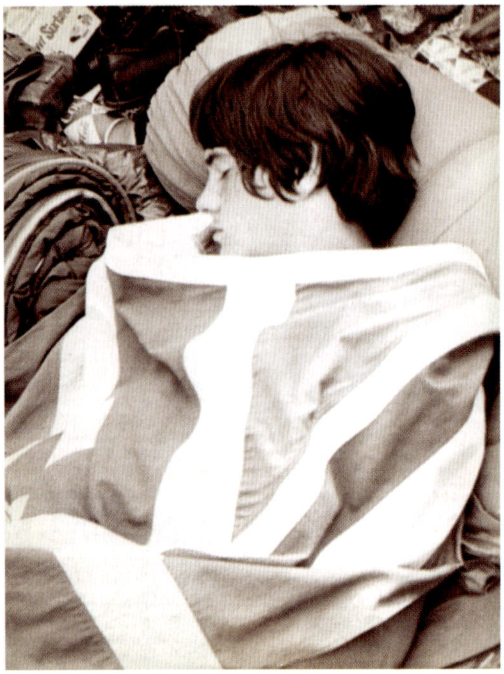

Dreaming of the British Invasion, a young Barry Beard naps at Dallas's Lee Park wrapped in a Union Jack. One of the most flamboyant glam-rock drummers in DFW, he later changed his name to Tyler Beard and metamorphosed into the "World's Leading Authority on Cowboy Boots." Courtesy of Barry and Teresa Beard.

Lady Wilde from Liverpool.
Courtesy of Vicky Williams.

The American Blues at Dallas's Satori House. Described in press reports as a "controversial young-adult ministry sponsored by area Presbyterians" in a "wildly-painted house at 2811 Oak Lawn," Satori House offered art, music, theater, and counseling from 1967 to 1969. On at least one occasion, shots were fired into the building by unknown parties upset with the presence of hippies. Courtesy of Trinity River Music.

with a country band. "She had healing powers and could make people well," adds her daughter. "Mom was bigger than life, amazing, charismatic."

The Warlocks—brothers Dusty and Rocky Hill with drummer "Little Richard" Harris—became the American Blues. The band presaged later tonsorial trends by dying their hair blue in 1966. "I got stopped by the police in Dallas once," Rocky Hill told *Star-Telegram* music writer Roger Kaye in 1979, "and the cop said, 'I just wanted to see what you was.' . . . The rednecks would give somebody with long hair trouble, but blue hair just sent them into a state of shock. They couldn't deal with that."

And when the American Blues started performing original material, Rocky added, "It was ridiculous. None of the clubs wanted to hire us in the Fort Worth-Dallas area."

Feed Your Head

Roger Kaye characterized the American Blues as "one of Texas's top psychedelic bands." A big part of the soundtrack of the sixties, of course, was music that probed the mysteries of the psyche and—to put it in terms as corny as some record promotions of the day—painted paisley rainbows everywhere. Some of these explorations, of course, were fueled by consumption of psychoactive substances. One tripper of the times claimed that, before LSD was made illegal in 1968, kids could buy it at the door on a five dollar "sugar cube" as they entered a Tarrant County teen canteen.

Other consciousness expansions were fueled by trippy light shows, ecstatic dance, and esoteric philosophy. Some of it was undoubtedly a little silly, some quite likely profound. Much paddled along rather harmlessly, somewhere in between.

Kenny Daniel, right, with his ’62 Strat, fronted the popular Kenny and the Kasuals. Courtesy of Kenny Daniel.

It takes a lot of psychedelic chutzpah to name your band the Visionary Indian Angels, but (left to right) Clay January (a.k.a. Lightning Rod), James Faretheewell, and Barry Gremillion were the real deal in Dallas, Texas. Another of their bands was called the Infamous Joy Urchins. Courtesy of Barry Gremillion.

Space Opera. Left to right: David Bullock, Scott Fraser, Philip White, Brett Wilson. Courtesy of David Bullock.

Kenny Daniel, guitar and vocals, squatting. The Kasuals included Lee Lightfoot, bass and vocals; David "Bird" Blachley, drums; Paul Roach, organ; Jerry Smith, guitar and vocals. Courtesy of Kenny Daniel.

"We were booked to open for Jefferson Airplane on November 1, 1970 at Daniel-Meyer Coliseum in Fort Worth," David Bullock recounted. "We previewed the concert on KFAD by playing a live recording of the set, done in our rehearsal room. Phil Cook, the program director at KFAD, was the emcee at the concert. People knew our music from the radio and from other shows but had never heard them played in this unusual format. The concert was a great success." Courtesy of David Bullock.

According to Kenny Daniel, front man of the sixties Dallas teen sensation Kenny and the Kasuals, his group's 1966 single, "Journey to Tyme," has been described as "the very first 'psychedelic style' recording." Other metro bands riding the psych wave—names harvested from a social media group about DFW music history—included Bloodrock, Neon Soul, The Fur Trapper Four, Electric Honey, Majic, Infamous Joy Urchins, The Country Roach Band, Southwest FOB, Heaven and Earth, Zorro and the Blue Footballs (who are said to have performed in their birthday suits), and many more.

One observer regarded Cowtown's Space Opera as "transcendent psychedelic country rock." This account by the band's David Bullock (guitar, flute, harmonica, vocals) appears to bear that out. "We were booked to open for Jefferson Airplane in 1970 at Daniel-Meyer Coliseum in Fort Worth," Bullock recalled. "For this concert we devised a set of music that would be totally seamless and continuous. Transitional elements, mostly instrumental, would tie the songs together and allow us time to reconfigure. It was a kaleidoscope of instrumental color and dynamics, from guitars/bass/drums to flute/grand piano/contrabass/vibes and everything in between."

The Briks' Pontiac hearse, filled with Vox Super-Beatle amps and other band gear. Courtesy of B. J. Hardesty.

Sixties Bands in Need of Spell Check

Somewhere along the flow of American popular music, it became a thing to invent alternative spellings for band names. This practice was especially prevalent, it seems, among sixties bands. In the Dallas-Fort Worth area, it resulted in such popular acts as Kenny and the Kasuals, The Briks, Styx and Stonz, the Sen-sa-shuns, The Motovators, and the Diminshuns.

"There was already a band called the Dimensions," explains James Anderson, who formed the Diminshuns at age thirteen. "So we thought it would be cool to spell it differently."

Other adventurous orthographers—Lee Hardesty of The Briks and Mike Nelson of the Sen-sa-shuns—demonstrated that a knack for creative spelling also indicated a knack for creative sound technology. The two lifelong friends, veterans of major Dallas lighting and sound provider Showco, founded Boomerang Musical Products in 1995. Nelson had gotten the original idea for the Boomerang Phrase Sampler in 1989 after searching for a quality looping device. Together they designed a prototype: "Made in Texas by musicians for musicians—a revelation in looping, with the ability to play back in reverse, change the speed of the playback, reverse your signal in real time and add in other effects while remaining easy to use."

The company's website remembers Lee's band The Briks as "the regional bad boy band. They wore the most black leather, had the longest hair, played the loudest and had the toughest attitude of all the Dallas area bands in the late 1960s."

Guys Five at the Colonial Club, Grand Prairie. Left to right: James Anderson, bass; Don Tomison, drums; C. B. Oliver, piano; Guy Parnell, guitar. Explaining the foursome's name, Anderson said, "We called the band Guys Five as a joke." Courtesy of James Anderson.

James Anderson's first band, the Diminshuns. The original group was a five-piece band, fronted by keyboard player Donnie LaGrone, who landed James a gig with Jimmy Reed. Donnie went on to tour with Jerry Wells and the Royal Lancers. Clockwise from left: Anderson, bass; Jimmy Herbert, lead guitar & vocals; Tim Cooper, rhythm guitar; Mike Davis, drums. Courtesy of James Anderson.

Seab Meador, far right, with one of his early bands, The Gentlemen, at the Studio Club in Dallas's Preston Center. Founded by Seab and Tim Justice, they played around Dallas from '64 to '68. When Seab left to join the Bridge, and then the Werewolves, local guitarist Danny Sanchez took over on lead. Justice wrote, "Like so many bands of this era, we had an incredible time playing music that we loved during a time when 16 to 18 year old kids were able to live lives far more mature than their ages implied. It was a unique time that will never be repeated." Courtesy of Jimmie Randall.

Seab Meador at a Werewolves show, Wooldridge Park, Austin, circa 1979. Gene Fowler took his ten-year-old son Nate to this show, and after seeing Seab perform, Nate decided he wanted to be a rock guitarist. Courtesy of Mark Ramsey.

Guitar Magic: "All the Girls Fell in Love with Him"

It may have started in Britain, where graffiti popped up in the sixties reading "Clapton is God," as testimony to the guitar skills of Eric Clapton. Whatever the source, "guitar god" as a term for highly skilled players of the instrument has definitely become a thing. Many a musician in the Dallas-Fort Worth area can be credited with qualifying for such a designation.

Seab Meador was one of the most remarkable guitarists to emerge from 1960s Dallas-Fort Worth. Debbie Hedges recalls that, while they were growing up in the Oak Cliff section of Dallas, "Seab sang and played 'Blue Suede Shoes' in the Mark Twain Elementary School Talent Show. All the girls fell in love with him that day."

Musicians appreciated his gifts as well. "He would dazzle you with the seemingly easy way he could tear notes from his guitar," remembers an early bandmate, bassist Jimmie Randall, "and still give you a knowing wink at his own presumptions that he still had much to learn."

Garage band scholars note that one of Meador's bands, The Gentlemen—heavily influenced by early Rolling Stones, Animals, Kinks, and Yardbirds—produced one of the genre's most important 45 rpm recordings, "It's a Cry'n Shame." Gentlemen drummer Tim Justice recalled that Meador "had a gaping hole in the middle of his Vox Super Beatle [amplifier] so that he could stick his guitar neck inside to get the fuzz tone" heard on the recording.

Seab Meador met his wife Judy Jergins in 1977, when she and some friends from Dallas saw a flyer taped to a New York City telephone pole announcing a show by the Werewolves, a Stones-y glam rock band from Big D in which Seab played

The incomparable Seaborn Meador. "He had his own look going on," said his wife, Judy Jergins, "kind of like Keith Richards, but he had his own style." Photo by Dennis Recla / Courtesy of Gloria Wilkes / BigD60s.

lead guitar. Though Judy described herself as having a fairly conventional appearance, there was immediate chemistry between the two.

"The Werewolves were quite a surprise to us," Judy says. "They were original, to say the least. The band had stage presence and one of the best guitar players we had ever heard. We all thought Seab was brilliant—there was no one else quite like him. And he had his own look going on, kind of like Keith Richards, but he had his own style."

Before the night was over, Seab said to Judy, out of the blue, "Let's get married." Soon, they were living together in Manhattan's legendary Chelsea Hotel. "Seab had a little desk in our room set up with a shrine of sorts. It included the Werewolves' second album, *Ship of Fools*, a picture of Edith Piaf in concert, copies of William Burroughs's *Naked Lunch* and other books that included biographies of Piaf and Judy Garland." The shrine spread to a nearby table, where Seab had set up a photo of The Fabulous Thunderbirds with his guitarist friend Jimmie Vaughan. "There were also five candles," Judy recalls, "one blue, green, white, red and yellow in front of the picture. They each stood for something, green for money, and so on. Seab had little rituals, things he would read out loud daily about wealth, power, peace of mind, and health. I guess you could say he was 'spiritual.'"

That staunchly independent aura of spirituality provided needed strength when cancer ended Seab's life so heartbreakingly early at the age of thirty-one on January 24, 1980. Judy was at his hospital bedside with fellow Werewolves and family. "We waited there until Seab took his last breath. I remember he opened his eyes and said, 'I love you all,' then shut his eyes and breathed a few more very slow breaths . . . and then he was gone."

"We dress this way to go to 7-Eleven"

The bohemian appearance of the hippies in the sixties was confusing enough for some of the more conservative residents of the metroplex. But the gender-twisting look of the glam rock crowd, especially evidenced in Dallas in the early 1970s, produced colossal stupefaction. Drummer Barry Beard, who in the 1980s would change his name to Tyler Beard and become known as the "World's Leading Authority on Cowboy Boots," recalled, "We dripped nightly in velvet, satin, shimmering lurex, snakeskin, and glitter. We were coiffed and made-up with chiffon and jeweled accoutrements. Were we pirates, pansies, or pop stars? We kept them guessing. Sure, we got heckled a lot for our androgynous outfits and outlook. A few feather boas were torn from our necks. A few beer cans were pelted at us, but overall the attitude that we were already stars seemed to create an invisible, impenetrable wall between us and the rest of the world."

Before they moved to New York, the Werewolves braved the redneck gauntlet on a daily basis as they strode through Big D in New York Dolls-y tough-guy-drag. As one Werewolf—perhaps bassist Buck Ballard—told the local *Buddy* magazine, "We dress this way to go to 7-Eleven."

And here again, Werewolves guitarist Seab

Seab Meador, when he was playing with a band called Dogfood. Notice the photo of the famous yogi, Paramhansa Yogananda, pinned to the grillcloth of his Marshall stack. Courtesy of Jay Taylor.

Dallas glam-rock heartthrob David Faulkner.
Courtesy of David Faulkner.

Valentine's Day with David Faulkner and the Toys, at Gertie's. Courtesy of Judy Blundell / David Faulkner.

Will Clay of the Toys also played in the Potatoes. ("We're the Potatoes from Dallas, Texas.") His favorite sax player was Eric Dolphy. Courtesy of David Faulkner.

Gary Myrick performing at the Agora Ballroom in Dallas. Proclaimed a "Texas Tornado" by Dallas's *Buddy* magazine, Myrick's early Dallas/Austin bands included Smiley, Slip of the Wrist, and Krackerjack. In the 1980s Gary Myrick and the Figures released three major label albums, and his song "She Talks in Stereo" appeared in the film *Valley Girl*. In the 1990s the guitarist formed the band Havana 3 am with former Clash bassist Paul Simonon. Myrick has also performed and/or recorded with such artists as Jackson Browne, Wilson Pickett, Stevie Wonder, John Waite, and Steve Jones of the Sex Pistols. Courtesy of Gary Myrick.

Jimmie Randall, originally from Duncanville, bassist for The Shadows, the Squires, Styx & Stonz, The Beefeaters, Smiley, Slip of the Wrist, Jo Jo Gunne, and the Dead Pyrates Society. Courtesy of Jimmie Randall.

Smiley, with Jimmie Randall, Gary Myrick, and Ben Watson. Courtesy of Gary Myrick.

Max Pageant, Dallas, early 1970s. Left to right: Joe Kennedy, Jack Morgan, Ben Watson, John Benoist. Ben Watson and John Benoist later went on to careers in painting and photography. Jack Morgan, a blazingly talented guitarist who studied with Seab Meador, later formed a group with James Anderson and Ty Grimes that was courted by major labels. "I've worked with a ton of guitar players," says Anderson, "but none inspired me like Morgan. The guy was phenomenal." Joe Kennedy logged some years in Vegas playing in a Stones tribute band. In 2009, Margaret Moser wrote about Joe's most recent band, the Dead Pyrates Society, in the *Austin Chronicle*, praising his "ragged vocals" and the "swagger [that made him seem] like Keith Richards' Texas cousin." Courtesy of Ben Watson.

Dallas's proto-glam band the Big Punks, with Jimmy McClellan, vocalist for Axcraft, Rockin' Sweet Nasties (with Robin Syler and Uncle John, etc). McClellan, who grew up in Phoenix with Vince Furnier (Alice Cooper) contends that the band's makeup and costuming influenced the stage get-ups of KISS. Larry McNenny at left. Courtesy of Jimmy McClellan.

Werewolves lead singer Brian Papageorge recalled in Andrew Loog Oldham's 2002 book, *2Stoned*, that the band recorded their second RCA album, *Ship of Fools*, on a yacht in the Florida Keys. Doing overdubs back home in New York, Papageorge recalled, Oldham wanted him to present a certain attitude in one of his vocals that Brian could not quite muster. "Right in the middle of trying to explain it to me for the umpteenth time he suddenly called a halt to the session and took me out to see *Saturday Night Fever* with John Travolta. All through the movie he was....telling me that's the attitude....We got back to the studio about midnight and I did the song in one take." Photo by Dennis Recla / Courtesy of Gloria Wilkes / BigD60s.

Superman's Girlfriend: Erin Arthur at the Hot Klub. "The Dallas Music Scene in those days was very small and had very little in common with the one that exists now," says Erin. "What it did have was raw energy and that sort of 'f*** the mainstream industry and those who support it' attitude, which is why an alternative scene happened in the first place. We all found the means by which to hear the sort of music that moved us at the time... we made it ourselves and had a hell of a good time doing it." Courtesy of Erin Arthur, photo by Jon Lacey.

Meador was a standout in style. Wife Judy Jergins recalls that in one NYC neighborhood, residents thought the musician was "the strangest thing they had ever seen. He carried around this red bag that had all this stuff in it, a can of Aqua Net hairspray, pens, writing tablet, inhaler, Jungle Gardenia, baby powder, wallet, address book, eye liner, aspirin, pink hairbrush with a long skinny handle, and other things. He was as bad as a woman."

At the same time, she found him "just so down to earth. It was so totally unexpected for someone who looked the way he did onstage—and offstage, as well. The make-up and the hair was the same, all the time."

Bucky Ballard played bass for the Werewolves, and, like Seab, left this world much too soon. Photo by Dennis Recla / Courtesy of Gloria Wilkes / BigD60s.

Werewolves' drummer Bobby Baranowski. Photo by Dennis Recla / Courtesy of Gloria Wilkes / BigD60s.

Often described as "amazingly underrated," the Werewolves' two albums came out on RCA in the late 1970s, produced by Andrew Loog Oldham, who had previously managed a British band called the Rolling Stones. Left to right: Brian Papageorge, Kirk Brewster, Seab Meador, Bucky Ballard, Bobby Baranowski. Courtesy of Gloria Wilkes.

While growing up in Dallas, Steve Miller's family friends included Les Paul and T-Bone Walker. Courtesy of John Lomax III.

Boz Scaggs (Wm. Royce Scaggs) attended St. Mark's in Dallas, where he became the vocalist for fellow classmate Steve Miller's band, the Marksmen, in 1959. He appeared on the Steve Miller Band's first two albums. Courtesy of John Lomax III.

Born in Dallas in 1947, Marc Benno played with The Doors, Eric Clapton, Stevie Ray Vaughan, Leon Russell, and Rita Coolidge. Seen here, center, with an early band, the Marc Benno Trio. Courtesy of Marc Benno.

"Hey hey we're (one of) the Monkees"

More than a few DFW area musicians of the sixties and early seventies headed off to the big time. Though a few years older, Michael Nesmith of the popular rock band-TV show The Monkees attended the same North Dallas high school as the authors. As did one Michael Lee Aday, who became better known to music fans as the hard rocker Meat Loaf. Aday has confessed to making up various stories about the acquisition of his stage moniker. In one version, a teenage Aday made a bet that a friend could drive his Volkswagen over Aday's head without causing significant injury. "Your head will look like meatloaf," the friend predicted. Aday's cranium survived intact, but the name stuck.

Born in Milwaukee in 1943, Steve Miller began playing professionally as a preteen while growing up in a musical household after the family had moved to Dallas in 1950. His mother was a jazz singer, and his physician father was such an adept amateur recording engineer that family friends included Les Paul, who became Steve's godfather and encouraged the boy to take up the guitar at age five. When Miller was nine, T-Bone Walker stood in the family living room and demonstrated his techniques for playing the guitar and doing the splits for the young guitarist. In the 1960s Miller became one of the Texas musicians playing bluesy rock in San Francisco, where a song from his third album, "Space Cowboy," became something of a moniker.

Plano was still a small farm community north of Dallas when Boz Scaggs moved there with his parents in the 1950s. He began playing cello at age nine. A year younger than Miller, Boz joined Miller's band the Marksmen when both attended the private school St. Marks. He also played Dallas folk clubs in an outfit called the Bacchanal Trio. Like many musicians, however, much of his education came over radio speakers, where he heard the sounds of Lightnin' Hopkins and Memphis Slim on Jim Lowe's influential WRR program, *Kat's Karavan.* T-Bone Walker's "Blues for Marili" especially resonated. "It was one of the sweetest things my ears had ever heard," he told San Francisco area music writer Ben Fong-Torres, "just perfection." He first came to the Bay Area in 1967 after rambling through Europe and India for a time. There, Boz joined his old pal Steve Miller's band for its first two albums before striking back out on his own.

The preferred ride for sixties bands in DFW...
Courtesy of Whit Snell.

The Denton Sixties Scene: "Smack Dab in the Middle of Rock 'n' Roll History"

In some ways, the lively university town of Denton, thirty miles north of Dallas and Fort Worth, is a smaller, less congested version of Austin, the self-proclaimed "live music capital of the world." The music school at the University of North Texas has long enjoyed national renown, and the thriving live music scene offers a diverse mix of local and touring bands most every night. Lesser known, however, is the town's importance as a music center in the story of the sixties.

Around 1965, members of several of North Texas's most active rock bands were living in Denton, including The Chessmen, The Jackals, and The Briks, who all lived and practiced in the same apartment complex. Felicity, featuring a young Don Henley and Richard Bowden, and The Beefeaters, which for a time included songwriter Gary Nicholson, also set up in the laid-back college town.

The groups were all managed by empresario wunderkind George Rickrich, whom the musicians affectionately called Fat George. Rickrich also managed the Campus Theatre, and in addition to his Bismark booking agency also issued 45 rpm recordings through the indie Bismark label. "For one of our first gigs in Denton," says Ron Dilulio of The Chessmen, "we played in the theater between showings of the movie *Get Yourself a College Girl.* Back then, there just weren't a lot of pop concerts like we think of concerts today. We were one of the first, and there were people lined up and down the street to see us."

Whit Snell, lead guitar for The Beefeaters, has vivid memories of the era's Denton scene. "By the end of my senior year of high school in 1966," he recalls, "we were ready to conquer the world. We planned carefully exactly how to execute our 'Big Fish Small Pond' theory. We would all attend the same university (then known as North Texas State) in small town Denton, and we would roll in, tight, and ready to play. Our flyers read, 'New British Sound Now Appearing Dallas Ft. Worth Area.' That seemed to work, at least for a while.

"Within a week of school starting we were playing on a large stage near the Student Union for the big 'Welcome to North Texas' street party.

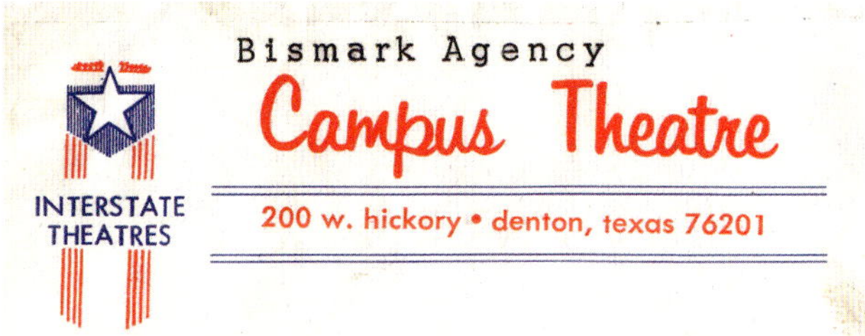

In the fall of '66 five young bands in Denton, Texas, signed with George Rickrich of the Bismark Agency. Of the twenty-three musicians in these bands, several literally changed the history of rock and roll. Don Henley, Jimmie Vaughan, Doyle Bramhall, Gary Nicholson, all sharpened their skills and started their musical journeys in the beer-drenched frat houses of North Texas and the dingy Dallas-Fort Worth clubs of the mid-60s. "The camaraderie of the boys of Bismark was unique," remembered Beefeaters guitarist Whit Snell. "They worked, played and often lived together for the next three years there in Denton, and friendships would develop that endure to this day." Courtesy of Cecil Cotten.

Whit Snell of The Beefeaters, in a scene that captures two of the sixties great themes, the British Invasion Union Jack flag and a shirt that reflects design elements of East Indian mysticism. Courtesy of Whit Snell.

George Rickrich's high school photo from Krum, Texas. Courtesy of Krum, TX Museum.

The Beefeaters, left to right: Dan O'Bannion, guitar and vocals; Mark Johnson, vocals; David McCullough, bass and vocals; Bill McCullough, drums; Whit Snell, guitar and vocals. Courtesy of Whit Snell.

The Beefeaters playing a frat party. Left to right: Whit Snell, Mark Johnson, Bill McCullough, Dan O'Bannion, David McCullough. Courtesy of Whit Snell.

Felicity, a talented group of musicians from Linden, Texas, at Honest Joe's Pawn Shop in Deep Ellum, circa late 1960s. Left to right: Mike Bowden, Jerry Surratt, Don Henley, Richard Bowden. Courtesy of Richard Bowden.

Mike Meroney, left, and Lee Hardesty made playing rock 'n' roll in the '60s look like more fun than the law allowed. Courtesy of Ron Dilulio.

The Chessmen appear on Channel 11. Left to right: Tommy Carter, Johnny Peebles, Doyle Bramhall, Robert Patton. Courtesy of Ron Dilulio.

The A-side of The Jackals' 45, "Love Times Eight," was recorded at Sumet-Burnet Studios by Bob Sullivan, who in addition to historic rock 'n' roll and country recordings, also engineered what many consider to be the first psychedelic recordings, with the 13th Floor Elevators. Guitarist Mike Neal remembers that Jimmie Vaughan, who was present at the session, loaned him his Gibson Fuzztone. As wild as the recording was, it didn't make it past the acetate stage, until twenty years later when it was released on Caped Crusader Records. The B-side, a cover of "Taxman," was from a '67 live radio broadcast from the Club Saracen, 1809 San Jacinto in Austin. KAZZ-FM's Bill Josey Jr. (DJ 'Rim Kelley'), along with his station-manager father Bill Josey Sr., were recording Texas 60s bands live from the Saracen, the Jade Room, the New Orleans Club etc. with a two-mic mixer system they developed, which allowed Josey Jr. to speak into one mic and capture the band with the other, sending it over a conventional phone line connecting them back to the radio station on a Saturday night! Pictured are the original Jackals. Left to right: Jay Kidwell, guitar (he was in the Navy so he wore a wig!); Mike Neal, guitar; J. B. Wyrick, drums; Billy Lawson, vocals; John Boware, bass. Courtesy of Billy Lawson.

SPINNING WHEELS
SKATING RINK
725 NORTH ELM — PHONE 382-8967 — DENTON, TEXAS

Sock Hop

EVERY SATURDAY NIGHT 10:15 P. M. TO 12:30 A. M.
$1.00 PER PERSON

Different well known area bands each week. Featuring "The Chessmen", "The Jackals", "Bondsmen", "Rogues", "Rox" (formerly "The Chaparrals") and others.
We invite only those who wish to participate in clean family fun. No drinking or bad conduct ever allowed and our rules are strictly enforced. Officer always on duty. Parents of children attending admitted free.

SKATING SCHEDULE

Tuesday, Thursday, Friday and Saturday Nights .... 7:30 - 10:00
Saturday and Sunday Afternoons .... 2:30 - 4:30
Friday Afternoon — Pre-Schoolers Thru 4th Grade .... 3:30 - 5:30

The Denton Skating Rink where all of the Bismark Bands played. Courtesy of Billy Lawson.

The Three Thieves hosted a Sunday afternoon jam session that was an immense amount of fun for Dallas 60s bands and friends. Also, it was the go-to after-hours club for famous bands visiting Big D. The Who, the Monkees, Hermann's Hermits, and others partied there. Billy Lawson, Jackals' vocalist, recalls, "The nicest bunch to come through were the Who. They were amazed that anyone in Texas had heard of them! When we played 'Boris the Spider' and 'My Generation,' they thought WE were cool!" Courtesy of George Gimarc.

A great Chessmen lineup with Doyle Bramhall, Johnny Peebles, Jimmie Vaughan, and Tommy Carter. Courtesy of Trinity River Music.

The Briks. Left to right: Mike Meroney, bass and vocals; Richard Borgens, guitar and vocals; Steve Martin, drums; Cecil Cotten, vocals. Upper right: Lee Hardesty, lead guitar and vocals. Courtesy of B. J. Hardesty.

The Briks. Left to right: Meroney, Hardesty, Cotten, performing at the Taylor Ranch. Courtesy of Jay Taylor.

Billy Lawson, Wm. Wms., John Talley of The Jackals, onstage at the Three Thieves. Courtesy of Wm. Wms.

The Chessmen at the Campus Theatre in Denton, January, 1965. Left to right: Robert Patton, Tommy Carter, Tommy Carrigan, Ron Dilulio. Robert drowned in a sailing accident in 1966. Courtesy of Ron Dilulio.

One of the only known photos of the interior of the Three Thieves and of the complete lineup of the last version of The Jackals: Ronny Sterling, bass; Phil Campbell, drums; Billy Lawson, vocals; Wm. Wms. guitar; John Talley, organ & guitar. Courtesy of Wm. Wms.

Felicity, outside of Ruby's Place, Deep Ellum, late 1960s. Left to right: Mike Bowden, Don Henley, Jerry Surratt, Richard Bowden. Courtesy of Richard Bowden.

We had long hair, bellbottoms, a big black Cadillac hearse with the name 'Beefeaters' painted on the side, and a wall of VOX Super Beatle Amps. Off to the side of the stage that night, arms folded and staring intently, was some other band. Band guys can always spot other band guys. They pointed at gear, whispered back and forth, and had longer hair than the crowd. But this group was a strange looking bunch. One looked like a bear. He was at least 6'2" and had a thick beard and had to weigh at least 250. Another of the band was probably less than four feet tall, and I would learn later that he had a rare dwarfism. He had on little short bellbottoms and had the longest hair, straight blond, of any of them. There was one other guy with them, and he was standard issue Rock 'n' Roll, except for a heavy East Texas accent. He said something like 'Ya'll are pretty good—where ya from?' I didn't know it, but I had just met someone who would change the course of my life. It would not be anything he would say or do, but instead would be another magical moment that would occur later that fall, much like what happened sitting in front of our old Zenith black and white, seeing the Beatles for the first time on the *Ed Sullivan Show*. It was a revelation."

It happened at the Denton Skating Rink. Snell found himself standing on the side of the stage, arms folded in the customary musician stance, awaiting a performance by Felicity, the band that had watched The Beefeaters from the side of the stage at the welcome party. "They looked out of place and I felt sorry for them," Snell recalls. "Then it was 'click, click, click' and a tight, crisp intro into Wilson Pickett's 'Knock on Wood' flooded the rink. Heads turned. Double bass drums pounded an irresistible dance beat, the likes of which I and those present had never heard, and Don Henley belted out, 'I don't wanta lose the good things . . . ' People rushed to the stage and dozens of teen girls on skates instantly fell in love with him. They were lined shoulder to shoulder along the four-foot-high stage, holding on to the rail, rolling their thin bare legs back and forth to the beat, spontaneously in unison. In less than two minutes he owned the place, and it was probably the coolest live performance I would ever see."

In another revelation that fall of 1966, Snell witnessed even younger virtuosity. The lead guitarist of The Chessmen, Robert Patton, had drowned in Lake Dallas the previous April, and the band found a replacement, whom Snell saw playing with the band at another Denton street party outside a university dormitory.

"The new lead player was some kid from Dallas who was a little short on equipment, playing an old, beat up blond Telecaster and no amp, so the Chessmen's bass player, Tommy Carter, borrowed my Super Beatle for the gig, and I came along for fun. The kid was skinny with long skeletal fingers and straight black long hair, WAY too long for a sophomore in a Dallas High School in 1966. You could not help but notice how clean this kid was. Not a pimple and the smoothest skin like a girl, and his jet black hair was thick and animated. He wore the Telecaster way down low. I remember thinking the girls are going to eat this guy up even if he can't play a lick. Turns out he could and his name was Jimmie Vaughan and he was sixteen. He was so good he even amazed himself. Sometimes he would be cranking out sounds and wails that would make Jeff Beck

Jimmie Vaughan's first band, The Pendulums, included Ronny Sterling and Phil Campbell. They may have been kids just having fun, as Vaughan has said, but this group of young Oak Cliff teens nurtured the seeds of some great Texas music. The Pendulums disbanded when Vaughan (standing at right) joined The Chessmen and Campbell and Sterling (along with later Pendulums member John Talley) became members of The Jackals. Later, Jimmie and Phil reunited briefly in an early version of Storm. "Doyle [Bramhall] sang, Jimmie played lead, Billy Etheridge on B3, me on drums—what a band!" marveled Campbell. Still later, Ronnie and Phil toured with Dallas bluesman Smokin' Joe Kubek. Courtesy of Rubye Campbell.

PARTIES DANCES CLUBS

THE PENDULUMS

FOR BOOKINGS

PHIL CAMPBELL
FE 7-0656

JIMMIE VAUGHAN
FE 1-5809

RONNY STERLING - FE 1-5938

Courtesy of Phil Campbell.

jealous and he would stare at his left hand on the neck and lean forward for a better look like 'how in the heck did I just play that lick?'

"Now, I was the lead guitarist for The Beefeaters, and I could play riffs from 'Johnny B Goode' and suddenly I realized I was in big trouble. I had played several times in front of these guys at venues we played together at and it was grueling. The Emperor had no clothes and Jimmie Vaughan knew it, but he was always gracious, complimentary and even taught me how to play 'Jeff's Boogie.' We would play nine weekends in a row in Austin, mostly UT frat parties and the New Orleans Club and Club Saracen, early Sixth Street. So did most of the other bands. We would meet up in Dallas and caravan down I-35 in our black Cadillac hearses, vintage mid 50s. These were a smart choice. Usually in great shape, with little miles and well maintained, they got us to the job and they were dirt cheap. Once we met up with the Chessmen at Jimmie's house, a little tract house in South Dallas, a neighborhood where dads with skinny pale legs and shorts pulled up too high, eyes squinting from a Chesterfield, would cook hotdogs on Sunday on a rusty Weber in the driveway. Jimmie's scrawny little brother Stevie Ray came out (I guess he was twelve or thirteen) and wistfully watched Jimmie load up and the Rock 'n' Roll Caravan slowly pull away. I can't forget this now and it seemed so trivial at the time. Someone onboard our hearse said, 'I heard Jimmie's little brother is a pretty damn good guitar player.' Sure, I thought, and it would be years later before I would remember that."

After experiencing performances by Don Henley and Jimmie Vaughan, Snell reckoned with the sinking feeling that rock 'n' roll fame and glory would, for him, prove unreachable. "From then on it pretty much became survival. Run the band like a business. Forget the original music. Show up on time. Dress sharp. And let the guy who writes the check sing 'Louie Louie.' It worked. What we lacked in talent, we made up for in pure business sense, and in a few weeks we were invited to go see Fat George."

George Rickrich, Snell recalled, "was the Godfather of the music scene in Denton. He and Charlie Hatchett from Austin controlled everything north of San Antonio all the way to the Oklahoma border. George's so-called real job was manager of the Campus Theatre. There, at the back and above the large, dimly lit balcony, was George's office for Bismark Agency, filled with

The Pendulums at the Beachcomber on Dallas's Lovers Lane. Their parents took turns driving the fourteen- and fifteen-year-old musicians to gigs. "At least this gets those drums out of the house for a while," said Phil's dad. Jimmie Vaughan's father worked briefly for Phil's dad at the Campbell-Rogers Office Supply, and the families often got together for a game of 42. "We practiced in my living room on Texas Drive," Phil recalled, "or in Ronny's garage on Poinsettia, or at Jimmie's house on Glenfield. I did all the singing. We played Battles of the Bands, Stockard Jr. High 'sock hops,' the Rocket Skating Rink in Cockrell Hill, the Flair in Oak Cliff. We were a 'novelty' not only because we were so young, but we were also good. We played from the heart even though we were doing covers—the usual stuff, Zombies, Stones, Kinks, Wipe Out, Jeff's Boogie, Jimmy Reed, Freddie King...." Courtesy of Donna Vaughan.

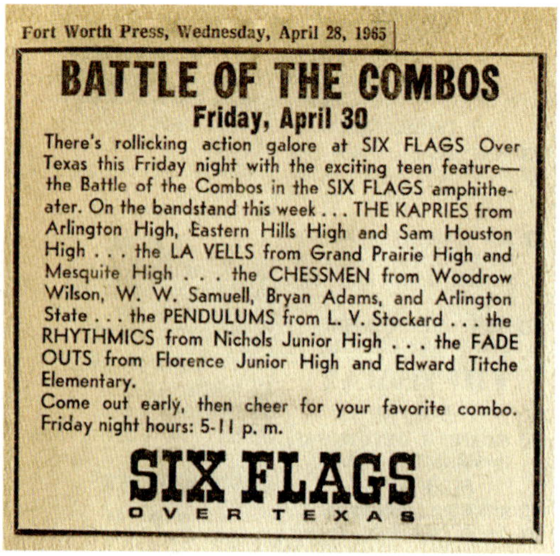

Fort Worth Press, Wednesday, April 28, 1965

BATTLE OF THE COMBOS

Friday, April 30

There's rollicking action galore at SIX FLAGS Over Texas this Friday night with the exciting teen feature—the Battle of the Combos in the SIX FLAGS amphitheater. On the bandstand this week . . . THE KAPRIES from Arlington High, Eastern Hills High and Sam Houston High . . . the LA VELLS from Grand Prairie High and Mesquite High . . . the CHESSMEN from Woodrow Wilson, W. W. Samuell, Bryan Adams, and Arlington State . . . the PENDULUMS from L. V. Stockard . . . the RHYTHMICS from Nichols Junior High . . . the FADE OUTS from Florence Junior High and Edward Titche Elementary.

Come out early, then cheer for your favorite combo. Friday night hours: 5-11 p. m.

SIX FLAGS
OVER TEXAS

This "Battle of the Combos" was shortly before Jimmie joined The Chessmen, and the rest of The Pendulums joined The Jackals—the only document to our knowledge showing The Chessmen and Pendulums playing on the same bill together. Courtesy of Andellyn Purvis-Hungerford.

Jimmie Vaughan, 1967, with The Chessmen at the Purple Onion. "His ability to play note-perfect versions of the day's hits helped make ... [The Chessmen] one of the city's top club and college-circuit draws," wrote Alan Paul in *Guitar World*. Vaughan told Paul, "I was making 300 bucks a week, more money than my dad .... Everyone else in the band was 21, and I was this little kid with attitude and a Telecaster. I knew all the licks." Courtesy of David Dennard.

movie posters, black and white photos of bands, food wrappers, and heaps of clutter, scribbled phone numbers, scratched out and circled dollar figures. On his desk were two or three black telephones, their rotary dials worn shiny silver from thousands of calls made by George's stubby fingers, and almost always a few large, beat-up metal film cans with masking tape that bore scribbled names like 'Bonnie and Clyde-REEL TWO.'

"George liked us because we were students and pretty squeaky clean. I liked George because we were allowed to watch the movie in the closed balcony after we delivered the check. There was a lot of talent in Dallas/Denton in 1966 and a few of the more talented were already experimenting with hard drugs and missing gigs or worse. He liked Henley also. Don was an English major and despite his East Texas accent (which he later lost in California), he was damn smart. Don and I would become good friends, and I would even play lead guitar for him for a few weeks one summer. I remember going with him as he rushed to deliver a term paper to the English building and another trip we made to school where he nervously went to check his grade. It mattered to him. By the spring of '68, our second year at North Texas, the war was hot and times were changing, as the song said. Instead of watching the Monkees and *SUMP'N ELSE*, the live Dallas teen dance show on TV, we were watching black and white footage of Hueys and soldiers smoking cigarettes, giving small sad waves to the camera. I didn't relate well to the hippie movement, and Don didn't either. It was like these guys drifted too far from the boat.

"Don was a musical genius and we were surrounded by musicians who had grown beards and smoked pot and stared at colors from oils on overhead projectors as they played songs that lasted for hours it seemed. Most of the old guard from Denton stayed with their roots, but Billy Lawson from The Jackals, the best soul singer EVER in my book, would get drafted and Cecil Cotten, lead singer of The Briks, enlisted. Our numbers dwindled. They both found themselves in Vietnam and both survived, miraculously. The bands that were left played in dirty dark clubs with blacklights and florescent psychedelic drawings on the walls, and music took on a whole new language that a lot of us didn't, or chose not to, speak. I hated the whole Woodstock scene. Looking back today I have a different take on the whole movement. Most of them believed in something. I believed in nothing, except not getting drafted, getting laid, a bartender who would give you a free beer on break, and having enough cash for a burger. I am not proud of that. It was the end of the British Invasion, and the beginning of the end of my rock 'n' roll years. Strangely enough, it was the beginning of Don's."

One day in 1968, the Felicity band members were in the Electric Rocking Horse boutique at 3305 McKinney Avenue in Dallas, looking for bellbottoms, when they spotted fellow shopper Kenny Rogers, whose chart-making band the First Edition was playing in Dallas. Jerry Surratt, Felicity's trumpeter-keyboard player, approached Rogers and asked him to come see them play at the Studio Club in Preston Center. It took a little persuading, but eventually Rogers not only caught their show but paid their way out to Los Angeles to record under the name Shiloh . . . which eventually, in Henley's case, led to The Eagles, whose greatest hits compilation is, according to some metrics, the best-selling album of all time.

The Fake Zombies

At least two groups of eager young Dallas musicians were preyed upon by unscrupulous Michigan promoters in the sixties and sent out across North America, touring as impersonators of the famous Zombies, an English band of the era that charted with songs like "Tell Her No" and "Time of the Season." The late Mark Ramsey, who toured with one iteration of the fake Zombies, left an illuminating account of the experience.

"During the psychedelic '60's," Mark wrote, "playing in a rock band became a cultural requirement." His own high school combo, Jukunda's Prism, had a female singer belting out "Somebody to Love" and other current tunes by the Jefferson Airplane, Buffalo Springfield, and the Byrds. After winning a Battle of the Bands competition at Will Rogers Auditorium in Fort Worth, the group relished the prize, the opening-act slot in a concert headlined by The Doors!

Soon, Mark met guitarist Seab Meador, when Seab's band played for a senior party at Mark's Grand Prairie High. "What a look he had," Ramsey remembered. "Jeff Beck hair, red flying V guitar, and a double-stack Marshall amplifier." Speaking to Seab at a break, Mark found him

The faux Zombies from DFW, with Seab Meador, Mark Ramsey, and two-thirds of the future ZZ Top. Courtesy of Mark Ramsey.

surprisingly friendly. Before long, he met drummer Frank Beard, an Irving High student, at a local pizza joint. He started hanging out with Frank, who seemed to know all the metroplex musicians. They caught Jimmie Vaughan at Yello Belly Drag Strip when the guitarist was just beginning to explore the blues.

Another night they went to see the American Blues. Talking with the band afterward, Beard learned that Little Richard Harris was leaving the group to move to San Francisco. Before long, Frank left his current band, The Cellar Dwellers, and joined the blue-haired Hill brothers. A half-century later, he's still playing with Dusty in that "little ol' band from Texas."

Seab was the first musician recruited by the promoters, then Frank and Dusty, and finally Mark. The enthusiastic young Texans set out in a van in the summer of '69 to tour the New World as the great Zombies from far across the deep blue sea. "When I found out that we were going to tour as the Zombies from England," Mark wrote, "I lifted an eyebrow, but I remember someone telling me that the manager had the legal rights to form a band to tour off of the Zombies great hit songs, as the original band had broken up." Amidst the hazy days of summer, the excitement of playing music for money under any conditions took over.

"Our set would feature hard-rock blues tunes that sounded as natural in Dallas as the Texas wind blowing hard from Mexico, but had little in common with the Liverpool sounds of the British Invasion," Mark continued. "Moreover, our sound would substitute The Zombies' melodic keyboard with Seab Meador's raunchy slide guitar." A couple of actual Zombies tunes were thrown in for good measure.

Surprisingly, audiences generally appeared to accept the young Texans as the English rock stars. One fan came backstage in Wisconsin and raised a stink, demanding to know what happened to

Widely considered the premier teen combo of the Fort Worth 60's garage bands, Larry and the Blue Notes released several songs on Major Bill Smith's Charay label, including three versions of their opus about the Lake Worth Goat Monster. Their live-in-the-studio recording of "In and Out" did not become a hit, but it oddly enough served as the B-side for five of their singles. Regardless, Ken Shimamoto described it as "a blast of white-knuckled Yardbirds-derived fury." The band toured Texas, playing teen clubs and TV shows. In one memorable career episode, an unscrupulous promoter sent the young Fort Worth musicians on a four-day, five-state tour as the Sir Douglas Quintet. Lead singer Larry Roquemore recalled that the Blue Notes were playing some three years before the Beatles' early gigs. "We were more of a rhythm and blues band," he told the press. "We opened for Ike and Tina Turner and played Bobby Bland and James Brown stuff. We'd go down to clubs on the Jacksboro Hwy., set up and pass the hat around. We were kids. We had no fear." The Blue Notes disbanded in '68. Left to right: Buddy Bates, Larry Slater, Mike Griffin, Larry Roquemore, and Dan Fletcher. Courtesy of Larry Harrison.

the keyboard player. When the boys were interviewed on a Canadian TV show, the incredulous host, detecting a slight, suppressed twang in the air, asked outright, "Are you guys from Texas?" But, wrote Mark, Canadian fans didn't seem to mind as the Texans won them over with "Rock Me Baby," "Black Magic Woman," and "Georgia On My Mind."

"That might have been our best performance," Ramsey recalled, "and to this day that ringing applause overshadows the many memories of the summer of '69. There was nothing fake about their response to our music. What they felt was real."

Meanwhile, Down in Cowtown

Scouting a little further west on the Trinity, another unscrupulous promoter sent the Fort Worth band, Larry and the Blue Notes, on a four-day, five-state tour as San Antonio's popular Sir Douglas Quintet. That episode was unearthed in the 1980s by Cowtown musicologists Larry Harrison and David Campbell. The team published their survey of 1960s Fort Worth garage bands, "Cowtown Calamity," in the underground magazine *Kicks* in 1984.

"One collector we called during our research," recalled Harrison, "said that Fort Worth

The business card of The Cynics, formed at Paschal High in '65, promised a "Boss Beat" by the cynical young band members, brothers John and Bob Rodriguez, Paul Christensen, Sandy Gregerson, and Ronnie Rambo. The Cynics battled other Fort Worth bands at Action A Go-Go and the Eastside, where, Larry Harrison wrote, "the owner threatened to toss them out if they played one more bad note." When a mortician's son became their soundman, a coffin came along as part of the deal, which The Cynics used as a stage prop. From time to time, a guest guitarist would pop out of the coffin to sit in, arisen from the world beyond. "In Fort Worth," added Harrison, "they enjoyed posing as the Yardbirds (who were in town at the time) for gullible Fort Worth kids who couldn't tell the difference between limey accents and Texas drawls." Courtesy of Larry Harrison.

Drummer Larry Larson, guitarist/vocalist Wesley Harris, and bassist Johnny Coleman started The Nomads in 1965. Bill Ham auditioned for lead guitarist and made the cut. Though the musicians were quite young—in ninth and tenth grades at the band's beginnings—they made a big impression on the Cowtown scene. "Of all the wild-ass Fort Worth '60s bands," wrote local chronicler Larry Harrison, "the barely teenaged Nomads were the wildest." Courtesy of Larry Harrison.

produced more good records in the garage-band period than any other city in the United States." Campbell theorized that such a concentration of creativity might have resulted from the power of pop, specifically Dr Pepper. "It had pure cane sugar in it back then, and David figures kids were hopped up on the stuff," added Harrison.

The article led to a three-volume compilation recording, *Fort Worth Teen Scene!*, featuring seventy-two songs recorded by dozens of local bands between 1964 and 1967. Engineer Phil York, who worked his mojo on garage band recordings produced by Major Bill Smith, recalled that most of the Trinity River musicians wanted their records to sound like the Beatles, a feat that sounded easy but proved quite difficult. Even T-Bone Burnett, York said, came walking into the studio with a box of Fab Four platters and proclaimed, "If I don't sound like these guys, I'm going to die."

Gary Carpenter of The Jades.
Courtesy of Larry Harrison.

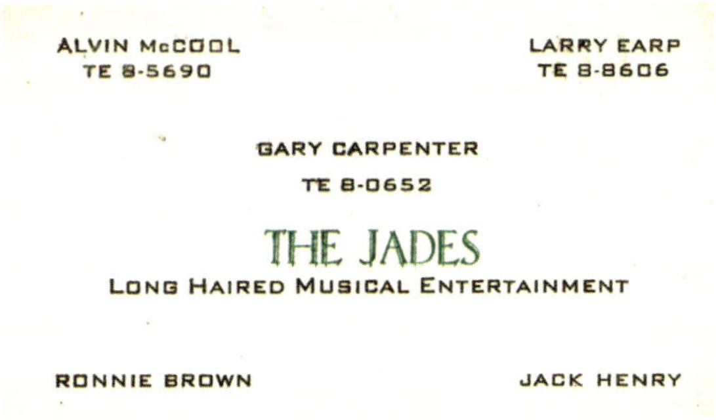

Courtesy of Larry Harrison.

KFJZ, the Fort Worth Jaycees, and Dr Pepper brought actress-singer Donna Loren to town to pep up a Battle of the Bands in December 1965. Larry Harrison theorized that "a contributing factor to the FW sound could be...DR. PEPPER. This tasty concoction still wasn't sold outside of Texas in the '60s and was being made in its most potent form during the garage band period. Super caffeinated and made with Imperial Pure Cane sugar ('It's quick dissolving!'), this pep pill of a soda pop was almost exclusively directed at kids via advertising and promotions (like sponsoring garage band clashes maybe?). Even the name Dr. 'Pepper' elicits a certain unconscious response that promises medicinal type stimulation for the user...uh, drinker. Getting hundreds of teens all jacked up on Dr. Pepper sulfate could only lead to one thing in the '60s: GARAGE PUNK!" Courtesy of Larry Harrison.

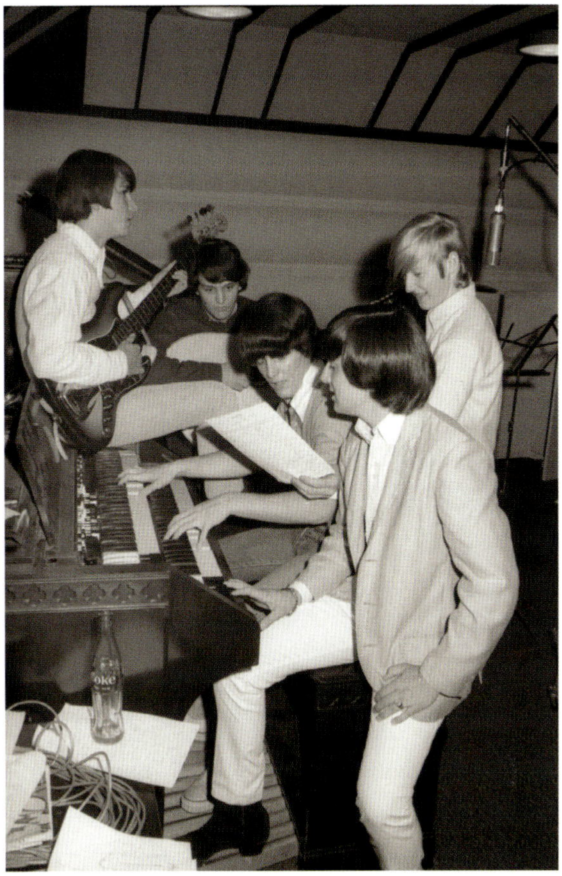

The Mods, recording in Phil York's studio. Younger than The Elite, The Mods from Paschal High were very talented musicians, made up of Edd Lively (lead guitar and vocals), Scott Fraser (drums and vocals), Danny Hawkins (guitar), Rick Finley (bass), and Don McGilvray (lead vocals). The Mods had a Beatles / Byrds fixation that they wore on their sleeves. They recorded their only single, "Days Mind the Time"/ "It's For You" (Cee Three records), when they were all only fifteen years old. Courtesy of Phil York / George Gimarc.

Fort Worth's Seventh Street Prophets, with James Ferris on keyboards. Courtesy of James Ferris.

The Elite became "Cowtown's answer to the Beatles," with Rodger Brownlee (vocals & guitar), Eddie Deaton (lead guitar), Bob Barnes (bass), and Bruce Lair (drums). The band was formed in early 1965, playing slumber parties and frat gigs for $5 a man, but they soon progressed to the Holiday Hop in Haltom City. In May 1965 The Elite took first place in the "combo" division of the Lion's Club annual "Stars of Tomorrow" talent show, competing against The Jades and the all-girl combo, Kandy and the Kandy Kanes. DJ Mark Stevens liked them, and gave them a spot on KFJZ's Teen A Go-Go. Stevens started having the boys play up the Beatles angle, calling them "Fort Worth's fab four" and "the band that looks like they just stepped off the boat from Liverpool." Courtesy of Larry Harrison.

Fort Worth's "All Girl Band," the Kandy Kanes, had a hit in '66 with "Hard to Tell," written by Frank Burkett, father of Fort Worth musician Hank Hankshaw. Reportedly formed as "a lark," the foursome (Candy Horn, Mylan Walker, Debbie Vorhes, Sherry Austin) became so successful, gushed entertainment reporter Elston Brooks, that the group "now has to get its schooling on the road." In this photo, the gals were getting ready to take their two guitars, organ, and drums on a tour all the way to Alaska. Courtesy of Michelle Dudley.

The Elite with their fan club. Courtesy of Larry Harrison.

The Visions (Gary James, Bruce Doshier, Billy Dalton, and Chuck Morgan), hailed from Mineral Wells. They cut three 45s while still in high school, "She's The Girl For Me," "Route 66," and "Humpty Dumpty," which were all released on the group's own Vimco label. After graduating from high school, they left for the Golden State, where they recorded for Uni and Warner Bros. They also performed in the TV drama *Run For Your Life* with Ben Gazzara, with costar & cool-guy/wildman (and *Buddy Holly Story* drummer) Don Stroud joining them onstage. The Visions (under a different name and with Joey Levine on vocals) played on a 1969 Buddah single called "Bubble Gum Music," written by ex-Strangeloves Bob Feldman and Jerry Goldstein. Courtesy of Larry Harrison.

The Barons, one of Fort Worth's best garage bands, were from Haltom High. The band was started by Ronnie Marcott (drums), Curly Benton (bass), and Don Babb (guitar). They were soon joined by Houston transplant, guitarist Johnny Nitzinger. Johnny used to write tunes in the Haltom gym with Larry Larsen of The Nomads, instead of suiting up for P.E. The Barons became a really tight live act. While other local combos played mostly covers, the Barons played original material, much of it written by Nitzinger. Marcott said the secret to their sound was that the whole band played through just two amps, with Johnny playing and singing through a Silvertone 610, purchased from a pawnshop, and Don and Curly playing through a bass-heavy Fender Bassman. Ronnie said most of the other local combos had new equipment and flaunted their new Vox Beatle amps, but when the Barons started playing and cranked up their used amps, the distinct sound it produced invariably drew teens, Pied Piper-style, to gather in front of the stage, where the shakin' and shimmyin' commenced. Left to right: John Nitzinger, Ronnie Marcott (in the back on drums), Don Babb, and Curly Benton. The boys are shown here at a department store in the sewing and fabric department. Courtesy of Larry Harrison.

Fort Worth Teen Scene! inspired *Teen a Go Go: A Little Film About Rock and Roll History* by Mark A. Nobles and Melissa Kirkendall. "The Beatles started something that inspired teens in this cultural backwater to form garage bands," observed a snarky Canadian reviewer, "learn a couple of chords and rock out the rest of the decade."

The late Brooklyn garage-band expert, Billy Miller, was more appreciative, noting in the film that "the Fort Worth scene had a very high batting average, with really, really good records, that will always sound good."

Battle of the Bands contests—held at roller rinks, recreation centers, and drag strips—were popular throughout the metroplex in the 1960s, but Fort Worth carport combos took the format to a whole 'nother level. A battle royale in the summer of 1967, held at the Box and cosponsored by KFJZ, was judged not according to crowd appeal or rock 'n' roll chops as perceived by industry experts but rather by how long each group of racket-making boys could stand and deliver the goods.

Five bands participated, including The Sundown Collection, Those Guys, The Chosen Few, The Restless Set, and The Extremes. The last group played for an extreme eighty hours and fifteen minutes but were disqualified by KFJZ disc jockeys for having "outside help" in their endurance performance. Judges and other contestants alleged that the group had been hypnotized, boosting their abilities as mere mortals.

Fancy Space: Johnny Nitzinger, guitar and vocals; Linda Waring, drums; Curly Benton, bass. Courtesy of Linda Waring.

Jerry Williams (bottom left) and one of his early DFW bands, the Epics. Courtesy of Andellyn Purvis-Hungerford.

"I got on with Jerry Williams like a house on fire," testified Eric Clapton in his autobiography. "He was an incredible, larger-than-life character who looked like Jack Nicholson and sang like Stevie Wonder....I really loved his writing. In fact, musically, I loved everything about him. He could be a little overwhelming in person, but that was entirely forgivable given the scale of his talent." Courtesy of Christian Williams.

Top prize of $500 in music equipment then went to The Restless Set, who despite their professed restlessness, managed to do their thing for an impressive seventy-one hours and fifteen minutes. Some sixteen thousand music lovers reportedly attended the marathon battle over the course of three days.

Fred Dobbs, who was working his way through the University of Texas at Arlington by performing as a magician and hypnotist, had been asked by The Extremes to attend the contest and possibly provide some sort of mind-over-matter assistance. Parents of The Extremes were so incensed by the disqualification that they threatened lawsuits if the decision was not reversed.

"I did hypnotize The Extremes," confirmed Dobbs in a phone interview some fifty-three years after the battle. "The bands took medically required fifteen-minute breaks every three hours. I would briefly put them under during the breaks, and when they came out, they felt as if they'd had six hours of sleep."

Rev. Fillmore & the Swingin' Flames! Left to right: Rev. Fillmore James, guitar; Weldon Ray Cleveland, bass; Frank Cagigal, keys; Joe Washington, drums; Freddie Cisneros, guitar. Courtesy of Freddie Cisneros.

Terry Hungerford and The Motovators!
Courtesy of Andellyn Purvis-Hungerford.

Garland band The Galaxies took home a lot of hardware from Yello Belly's Battle of the Bands. Courtesy of Phil York / George Gimarc.

Dallas radio station KBOX sponsored Battles of the Bands at Yello Belly Drag Strip. Courtesy of George Gimarc.

Howard Reed, lead guitarist with Gene Vincent's Blue Caps, at a Yello Belly Drag Strip Battle of the Bands in May 1958. Howard taught guitar at McCord's Music in downtown Dallas, did lots of local studio work, and played the *Big D Jamboree*. Courtesy of David Dennard.

Emcee at the Yello Belly Drag Strip Battle of the Bands. Courtesy of Carter Buschardt.

The Galaxies mix it up with a live audience. Courtesy of Phil York / George Gimarc.

Larry McNenny of the Styx & Stonz, at the Shamrock Roller Rink. Courtesy of Jimmie Randall.

Floyd Dakil formed his Combo in '63 with fellow Highland Park friend Andy Michlin and three Thomas Jefferson High School friends: Ronny Randall, guitar; Terry Billings, bass; and Geoff West, drums. In '64 they won a Battle of the Bands at Lamar Hunt's Pit Club at the Bronco Bowl, where they became the house band. They recorded their hit song, "Dance, Franny, Dance," live at the Pit, with several hundred teenage fans, whose synchronized clapping can be heard on the 45. Left to right: Chris Brown, Floyd Dakil, Dennis Mills, Ronny Randall, Andy Michlin. Courtesy of Phil York / George Gimarc.

The Chaparrals began in '64, founded by four North Texas State freshmen. By '66, they were the house band for local clubs such as the Disc A Go-Go and the Three Thieves, where they opened for the Music Machine, the 13th Floor Elevators, etc. They left for California in '67, but disbanded in '68 in San Francisco. Drummer Steve Karnavas stayed to become the drummer for Benny, Cecil and the Snakes, consisting of Briks' vocalist Cecil Cotten, Wig and Jackals' guitarist Benny Rowe, and Keith Ferguson on bass. They were the house band for a while at the infamous Rip-Off Press and Zap Comix Warehouse parties. Courtesy of Jamie Bassett.

Louann's, the premier musical venue for the Dallas area, founded by Louann Bovis in 1939. Everyone from Woody Herman, Harry James, Guy Lombardo, and Lawrence Welk to Jimmy Reed and Jeff Beck played there. Courtesy of Andellyn Purvis-Hungerford.

The Rogues onstage at the Pirate's Nook in Dallas. The Rogues were: Wirt "Stitch" Davis (who later joined the Novas), Rusty Dealey, Mitch Gilbert, Doug Bailey, and Mike Ritchey. "The Tuff Sound for Parties and Dances." Courtesy of Janice Ivey / BigD60s.

William Ware's Pirate's Nook, 4422 Elm St., Dallas. Courtesy of Jamie Bassett.

The Chaparrals onstage at the Pirate's Nook. Courtesy of Jamie Bassett.

After Lu Mitchell, shown here at her home in Farmers Branch, moved to the metroplex in 1949, Dallas folk music scholar Hermes Nye inspired her to take up the guitar. She helped establish the Dallas Folk Music Society in 1959. She wrote more than three hundred songs, including one about President John F. Kennedy, and her oral history testimony about JFK and that tragic day in Dallas is archived at the Sixth Floor Museum. The *Dallas Observer* dubbed her "the musical version of Molly Ivins." Courtesy of Sean Mitchell.

The Excels, performing on the streets of Van Alstyne, began in '63 in McKinney, TX, formed by brothers James and Danny Goode, along with Gibson Harris on drums, and Roger Bennett on lead guitar. Ron Vermillion took Roger's place when he was drafted. Along with Howard Reed (a member of Gene Vincent's Blue Caps), Ron taught guitar at McCord's Music downtown. Howard also became the band's booking agent. The Excels played Louann's, frat parties at SMU & TCU, the Red Jacket, the Pirate's Nook etc., as well as a tour with the Ventures. Courtesy of James Goode.

The Excels recorded "Walkin' the Dog" and "Let's Dance" in '65 at the Clifford-Herring Studios in Fort Worth. Excels rhythm guitarist James Goode was inducted into the Rockabilly Hall of Fame in 2006 for "Walkin' the Dog." Courtesy of James Goode.

One online review of their *Sump 'N Else* recordings summed it up. "By 1968 The Novas were unquestionably the best band in Dallas, combining superb musicianship with unearthly harmonies, mixing great originals with tasteful covers of the Beatles, Byrds, Hollies, Yardbirds and more." Taken at Minsky's Music, left to right, John Salih, Uncle Al Minsky, Gary Madrigal, David Dennard, and Dave Brown. Courtesy of David Dennard.

Ace Song Service, clockwise from lower left: Charles Barbosa, Rusty Burns, Phil Looney, Ray Cobb; center: Keno Sharb. Burns, son of a c&w musician and guitarist since childhood, played the Cellar circuit from 1967 to 1973. He later toured with Point Blank. Cobb's mother, Margaret Cobb, wrote "Hey Baby!" for Bruce Channel, and the Ace guys recorded their own version in 1970, produced by Marvin Montgomery and engineered by Phil York. Channel later added his own vocals to the track, and Major Bill Smith released it in England. Courtesy of Phil Looney.

Vivian Thompson and fellow folk artist at The Rubaiyat, 1969. The "first coffee house in Dallas," The Rubaiyat provided a venue for the budding folk scene from about 1965 to '72. A young Ray Wylie Hubbard played there occasionally as part of a folk trio called Three Faces West after the John Wayne movie, along with B. W. Stevenson, Michael Martin Murphey, Lu Mitchell, and many others. James Anderson remembers playing there with fellow downtown County Community College musician Mickey Raphael. Courtesy of Vivian Thompson.

The Shadows, 1964, Duncanville. Top to bottom: Mike Holt, Jimmie Randall, Jim Funderburk, Jerry Williams. "We didn't know any bass players—I got my first bass right after this photo was taken in my parents' living room," says Randall, who holds an Airline guitar from Montgomery Ward's. The other two were Silvertones from Sears. Courtesy of Jimmie Randall.

Carter Buschardt, drummer for Blackbird, Brat, Blake, Birth, Cartoons, Flag, The Noblemen, The Pork Chop Revue, Rosco, Sugarcane, Thunderbird, and many others. Courtesy of Carter Buschardt.

The Farlow Brothers: Big Sonny Farlow, Ty Grimes, and Richard Farlow. The Farlows dominated the club scene in Dallas for a good while. Rocky Athas, upon hearing them for the first time, exclaimed, "You guys are 'Texas Roots Rock 'n' Roll!'" Ty Grimes has enjoyed an illustrious musical career, touring with Ricky Nelson's Stone Canyon Band (playing Carnegie Hall to four encores) then joining Captain Beefheart's Magic Band. After that he began drumming for Tim Weisberg, then moved to Dallas to play with his old El Paso friends the Farlow Brothers. Courtesy of Ty Grimes.

The Styx & Stonz at SMU's Moody Coliseum, 11-12-67, opening for the Mamas and Papas. Courtesy of Jimmie Randall.

Carter Buschardt, drums and vocals, with Blake at Lee Park, Dallas. Courtesy of Carter Buschardt.

With Marshall stacks, Flying V, and striped bellbottoms, Rocky Athas performs with Lightning at Lee Park. Known as the Malice from Dallas, among other soubriquets, the ace guitarist has recorded and/or toured with Buddy Miles, SRV's Double Trouble, Joe Walsh, John Mayall, and many others. Courtesy of Carter Buschardt.

Bruce Bowland, vocalist extraordinaire for the legendary Texas band Krackerjack, was also a founding member of the Texas Sheiks, with Jack Morgan, Uncle John Turner, and Keith Ferguson. "My mother took me to see Bo Diddley, Lloyd Price and LaVern Baker when I was 9; from that point forward I knew I wanted to be a singer." Photo by Lewis Lee.

"Locals Fear Invasion," proclaimed one headline in advance of the Texas International Pop Festival, held in Lewisville, just north of Dallas, in late August, 1969, shortly after the more famous fest in Woodstock, New York. Others read, "Cooperative Spirit Pervades at Pop-In," "Peace, Love, and Rock 'n' Roll—Texas-Style," "Strange Sights, Groovy Sounds in Lewisville," "Youths Live as Families at Festivals," "Drugs Mar Pop Festival." Though the town's mayor supported his actions, the chief of police resigned after locals felt he'd not been severe enough in arresting festival-goers for nudity, drug use, and noise. One young California girl confided that she'd been nervous to come to Dallas due to the city's reputation after the JFK assassination. Another attendee, a former New Yorker who quit his advertising job to live in New Mexico's "Hog Family" commune, who wore a necklace made of teeth, told reporters the Lewisville site was "cleaner, prettier, and more pleasant" than the Woodstock concert location. Two "young, hippie-type English women" were held for mental evaluation after unfortunate reactions to LSD. "Young people assembling to hear music is one thing," sneered one editorial. "Young people assembling in unspeakable costumes, half-naked, barefooted, defying propriety and scorning morality is another." Produced by Angus Wynne and Jack Calmes, the fest drew somewhere between 60,000 and 120,000 people. An original TIPF poster, like the one shown here, went for $3,800 at auction in 2012. Courtesy of Tom Kreason / Texas Musicians Museum.

Courtesy of George Gimarc.

Texas International Pop Festival producer Angus Wynne III in action with the latest communications devices circa 1969. Courtesy of University of Texas at Arlington Special Collections.

Courtesy of Tom Kreason / Texas Musicians Museum.

It was something of a homecoming when Sly and the Family Stone performed at the Texas International Pop Festival. Born in Denton as Sylvester Stewart in 1944, young Sly moved to California with his family at an early age. Raised in a deeply religious family, young Sly performed in the gospel tradition before forming the powerhouse funk band he brought to Tex Pop. Courtesy of George Gimarc.

The Contenders, photographed at the iconic Good Luck service station off Lamar, just south of downtown Dallas. Left to right: Jack Morgan, lead guitar; Little Brucie "Butane" Bowland, vocals; Mark Hamilton, drums; Will Robinson, keyboards; Darrell Strealey, bass. Courtesy of Mark Hamilton.

The Mystics, an Oak Cliff band, playing in Keist Park. Before they were the Mystics, when they attended Storey Jr. High, they were called The Glory Tones. Members included Ron Jobe, vocals; David Mitchell, bass; Robert Farris and Danny Fugate on guitars; and Glenn Struble on drums. Blocks from the childhood home of Stevie Ray and Jimmie Vaughan, Keist Park is the site of a sculpture commemorating the brothers. Courtesy of Alan Struble / BigD60s.

Dr. Broccoli: David Hill, guitar; Steve Wilson, vocals; Patrick Keel, drums; David Dennard, bass; not shown, Neal Caldwell, Wurlitzer keyboards. Later in life, Dennard and Hill played and recorded together in Jackpot, with Bruce Bowland on vocals. Courtesy of George Gimarc.

NCM ("Non Compos Mentis" – "not of sound mind") at the Hot Klub, opening for Gary Myrick and the Figures, 12-19-81. Formed in late '79 by members David Hill, Neal Caldwell, and Randy Caldwell. Neal also founded the VVV record label and record store on Lovers Lane. "An alternative to alternative record stores," it featured full racks of Jamaican reggae. Many local bands recorded on the VVV label, such as the Telephones, Bobby Soxx, and the Fort Worth Cats. Courtesy of George Gimarc.

The Nervebreakers at the Longhorn Ballroom, opening for the Sex Pistols, January 10, 1978. Left to right: Barry Kooda, Tex Edwards, Carl Giesecke, Mike Haskins. Though a press report at the time said some 1,800 tickets were sold, Barry Kooda has met thousands more who say they were there. "I just came to see the weirdos," one eighteen-year-old non-punk told reporters, "and I'd better get $3.50 worth of weirdos." Courtesy of T. Tex Edwards.

"Cowtown Cool!"

Charles Christy and the Crystals, seen here at Omar Khayam's in Fort Worth, had a regional hit in the midsixties with "Cherry Pie." Billed simply as Christy, the frontman had a comeback in the eighties when Major Bill Smith and others released his recordings in Europe. When Major Bill returned from the 1983 International Music Show in London, he rhapsodized to music writer Roger Kaye, "They think Charles Christy is going to be a Tom Jones, Engelbert Humperdinck, Cliff Richard, and Elvis Presley all rolled into one." Courtesy of Ron Dyer.

Teen Beats, 1963. Left to right: Terry McEachern, rhythm guitar; Jimmy Dodd, saxophone and vocals; Mart Brown, drums; Doug Morris, lead guitar; Mike Neal, bass; Nelda Caine, vocals (not shown). Courtesy of Mike Neal.

The Jokers: Charlie Mitchell, bass; Joe Schrieber, drums; Don Kappel, sax; Arvel Strickland Jr., guitar. Arvel grew up a few blocks from Jacksboro Hwy. He said, "I guess I played every place on that highway that would hire a white boy playing the blues—The Rocket, The Skyliner, The Sands, The Spot, The Chateau, Double Bar, Crescent Club, Casino Ballroom...." Courtesy of Charlie Mitchell.

Deploying enough talent for a full band, Homer Henderson is known for tunes like "Picking Up Beer Cans" (which someone called "the greatest country song that George Jones never wrote") and "Lee Harvey Was a Friend of Mine." Re. his Oswald opus, cowritten with Jay Cotton, Homer has said, "I think we wrote most of it while we were driving around drinking Slurpees and smoking weed. We'd pass by Oswald's house, the Texas Theatre, and Marsalis Avenue in Oak Cliff, where Jack Ruby had lived. Thirty years ago people didn't give a damn about it, but we knew all those places." The song has reportedly been covered by Oswald's old girlfriend, Judyth Vary Baker. "Lee Harvey was a friend of mine," Homer sang. "He used to take me fishin' all the time. He used to throw the ball to me when I was just a kid. They say he shot the president, but I don't think he did." Courtesy of Homer Henderson.

The young Homer Henderson with his Esquire guitar. Homer's first band, at Richland Hills Junior High, was The Moths. In addition to being a takeoff on The Beatles, Moth stood for "Men of the Hour." The boys crafted microphones from radio speakers and cymbals from garbage can lids affixed to broom handles stuck on Christmas tree stands. Courtesy of Homer Henderson.

Courtesy of Homer Henderson.

Housed in a former bowling alley at 3300 E. Lancaster, Panther Hall hosted rock acts as well as country-western stars. The TV program, *Panther-a-Go-Go*, was also broadcast from the venue, complete with go-go dancers. Courtesy of Andellyn Purvis-Hungerford.

Courtesy of Carol Galt.

A young Robin Syler with a bass guitar (below). An older Robin with a Flying V (above right). And full-Texas-mode Robin with a six-shooter and a hat (above). "Robin might have looked fragile in his later years," wrote Fort Worth writer and musician Ken Shimamoto, "but he was still larger than life, a big persona with the flamboyance of a Jerry Lee Lewis or a Screamin' Jay Hawkins. He dressed the part in cowboy shirts of his own design that combined eye-catching swatches of color with retro/ghetto-fabulous leopard or tiger patterns." Courtesy of Carol Galt.

Courtesy of Carol Galt.

Hank Hankshaw at the Blue Bird. Courtesy of Hank Hankshaw.

"You must be weird or you wouldn't be here," read the slogan painted on the walls of the Cellar, a notorious, late '50s and '60s club that established outposts in Fort Worth, Dallas, Houston, and (briefly) San Antonio. Owned by former race car driver Pat Kirkwood, whose father, W. C. "Pappy" Kirkwood, operated the equally notorious 2222 Club on the Jacksboro Highway, the Cellar could stay open 'til 6 a.m. because it didn't sell alcohol. Some recall a sense of freedom at the joints, others a sense of danger. Gary Myrick says a bullet whizzed by his head one night onstage. Jack Ruby often prowled the Cellar hoping to recruit new dancers for his Dallas strip joint from the barely clothed waitresses. It's said the Secret Service lurked in the Fort Worth Cellar the night before the Kennedy assassination. Musicians who often performed at the Cellar included Arvel Stricklin, Jack Estes, Adrian Watts, Cannibal Jones, John Nitzinger, G. Tiger, Guy Parnell, and the Knightbeats. They were joined by the Cellar Dwellers (who played lots of Beatles tunes), the Neurotic Sheep, and the Geeks. Brothers Dusty and Rocky Hill and drummer Frank Beard also played at the clubs. In 2013, Giles McCrary released the Cellar documentary film, *You Must Be Weird or You Wouldn't Be Here*. Courtesy of Rick Benedict.

Courtesy of Rick Benedict.

Singer, songwriter, and drummer Doyle Bramhall joined the Chessmen in '66, along with Jimmie Vaughan, while still in high school, opening for Hendrix when he played Dallas. In the '70s Doyle formed the Nighcrawlers with Marc Benno and Stevie Ray, for whom he wrote "Life by the Drop" and "Dirty Pool." He also had a power trio with fellow Fort Worth friend Robin Syler and bassist Alex Napier, called The Millionaires. A massive Texas talent with a heartful of soul, Big D passed away of natural causes in Alpine TX, November 11, 2011. Courtesy of Carol Galt.

Mace Maben, of the Viscounts, Courtship and Texas, which recorded an LP for Bell Records. According to one critic, Mace had "an understated but undeniable stage presence." Courtesy of musicandartsagogo / Trinity River Music

"Far Out Wedding Set in Beatnik Hangout" read the *Star-Telegram* headline when rockabilly great Johnny Carroll, shown here at the Fort Worth Cellar, where he served as entertainment booker and often performed himself, married a waitress called "the Overaged Lolita" in 1960. Carroll wore dark glasses and a beret for the nuptials, which took place at midnight. Courtesy of George Gimarc.

"I'm the Fort Worth Cats' biggest fan!" proclaimed the notorious Bobby Soxx (dancing in foreground). Cat Mike Neal, (guitar, vocals, former Jackal—shown here with his '64 Jazzmaster) said the band sounded like "a cross between the Ventures and the Sex Pistols." Richard Fenner, owner of the Fort Worth punk club Zeros, told Neal that he opened the joint so the Cats would have a good Cowtown venue. Other Cats were David Daniel, bass/vocals; Johnny Willett, drums; John Siebman, guitar/keyboard/vocals. Its name echoing the legend of Fort Worth as "panther city," the band recorded two albums and an EP. Other Fort Worth-bred musicians prominent in Texas's punk/New Wave scene included cinema maven Tom Huckabee of the Huns and Steve Marsh of Terminal Mind. Courtesy of Mike Neal.

The Fort Worth 60's crowd has maintained an unbroken tradition of gathering in Trinity Park annually to celebrate the sounds of the sixties. Designed by John Allen. Courtesy of Rick Benedict and musicandartsagogo.

Ceremony

Erykah Badu's Dealey Plaza Return

"Self-described as 'a mother first,'" begins Erykah Badu's "about" statement, "Badu is a touring artist, producer, dj, director, activist, holistic healer, doula, veggie, bgirl, observer, hustler. . . . "

The Dallas performer with 3.4 million social media followers was born in Big D eight years after President Kennedy was slain on city streets. Osmosis, surely, has informed her perspective on the psychic wound inflicted on area artists who lived and witnessed on that day. Testifiers to the anguish and confusion, the blessed love and bitter hate, the bruised grace that struggled for breath.

March 17, 2010. Erykah Badu parks a 1965 Lincoln Continental along the president's parade route and begins walking toward Dealey Plaza, removing layers of clothing, symbolically stripping away the names and faces that populated the legacy of fear baked into the landscape. "Welcome to Dallas, Mr. President." John Birch Society. Mink Coat Mob. Mafia. Klan. H. L. Hunt. Gen. Edwin Walker. Demon money. "Monte Carlo on the Trinity." One by one, they fall away.

Naked and new, as she was when she entered this life, she falls to the earth near the place where John's last moment was held so close. There. At the vortex of "Murder Most Foul."

Family Album

The authors and their families have deep musical roots in North Texas, with branches that continue sprouting new and adventurous sounds today.

Hugh Fowler (1922-1979), seen here on trumpet, led a big band and operated an entertainment booking agency. In the late 1940s/early '50s, he also served as musical director of KRLD Radio and TV. In the late 1940s he partnered with *Hillbilly Hit Parade* and *Cornbread Matinee* deejay Hal Horton in Metro Music publishing company, and around 1966, he "booked" Gene Fowler, William Williams, and Deborah Riddles as "rent-a-hippies" for a hippie-themed party in Highland Park. Courtesy of Gene Fowler.

Hugh Fowler Jr. (1948-2016) had a popular dance band in the late 1960s and early '70s. Courtesy of Gene Fowler.

The last showbiz cigar. Courtesy of Gene Fowler.

The American Fuse. Left to right: J. T. Dayton, Nate Fowler, Clint Phillips, Kinley Wolfe. Courtesy of Nate Fowler.

Left, Hank Thompson; right, Gene Fowler. Courtesy of Gene Fowler.

Gene Fowler played the family instrument in elementary and junior high school. He interviewed Hank Thompson, whose early songs were published by Metro Music, for his book *Border Radio* in Christoval, Texas, circa 1986. Active as a performance artist since the 1960s, Gene began singing in shows in 2002. Courtesy of Gene Fowler.

The Williams Boys, 1930s, Paris, TX. Top, left to right: Gilford Thomas Williams, Albert Grover Williams, Ambrose Lee Williams; bottom left to right: J. R. Williams, Robert Jr. Williams, Hubbard Williams. Five brothers who travelled around Texas and Oklahoma in the early '30s. Surviving brothers stated that Ambrose "sometimes played with Jimmie Rodgers, who wanted him to travel with him and be his main guitarist, but Lorene (Ambrose's wife) wouldn't stand for it because she was tired of having to raise three kids all by herself." Shortly thereafter, Ambrose died of typhoid, from contaminated well water. Courtesy of Wm. Wms.

The Intruders, at the Edward H. Cary Jr. High Talent Show. Courtesy of Wm. Wms.

Ronnie Letot, William Williams, and Jonathan Williams. Courtesy of Wm. Wms.

William, playing with the band Bomber Spur at a Fort Worth club. Photo by Lewis Lee.

Here's the son of one of the Williams Boys, George Albert (second from right) with one of his own bands. Many of the sons and grandsons of the Boys continued the family's musical tradition in North Texas. Courtesy of Wm. Wms.

William playing lead for a country band at a Granbury honky-tonk. "This three-pickup Danelectro twelve-string guitar was bequeathed to me by my friend, the great slide guitarist and guitar tech David Hill. We offer *Metro Music* especially as a tribute to the memory of all these amazing musicians and dear friends who have gone on before us." Photo by Lewis Lee.

Acknowledgments

For assistance with this project, the authors send immense thank-yous to Lewis Lee, Joseph Thomas Chenoweth, Stephenville Historic House Museum, Donna Donnell, Carolyn Wills, Linda Jo and Scott Barker, Pat Boatright, Pat Bywaters, George Gimarc, David Dennard, Pauline Marceleño Laws, Debra Petton Bell, Eve Bowen and Hill College Library, Gerard Daily and Bill Mecke at Record Town, Competition Music, Guy Lawson, James Pennebaker, Rick Benedict and musicandartsagogo, Carrie Kordonoway, Larry Harrison, Kevin Coffey, Sara Pezzoni and the University of Texas at Arlington Special Collections, Fort Worth Public Library, Dallas Public Library, Erath County Genealogical Society, Bill McClung, Marshall Wyatt and Old Hat Records, Michael Lee Garrett, the Albuquerque Museum, Atlanta (TX) Public Library, Scott Tanner, Dolores McHargue, Doug Hall, Don O, Sumter Bruton, Jay Brakefield, Ted Tucker, Donna Vaughan, James Anderson, Brandy Herbert, Linda Waring, Carol Galt, Mike Buck, Jim Colegrove, Johnny Case, Phil Strawn, Steve Bonner, Laura Lynch, Terry Williams, Black Academy of Arts and Letters, Jewell Blanton Kelly, Chloe Webb, Nancy Gillis, Mike Nichols, Tarrant County Archives, Joe Whitney, The Portal to Texas History, James Rovitto Jr., Ronald Shannon Jackson, Carl Sidle, The Wittliff Collections at Texas State University, Tracy Pitcox, Charlie Mitchell, Jimmy Capps Jr., Dallas Mexican American Historical League, Juanita Nanez, Albert Valtierra, Crazy Chuy Hernandez, Aurora Vega Mata Burciaga, Carlos Saenz, Scott Tucker, Andellyn Purvis-Hungerford, Phil York, Betty Torres, Gayle Thomas, Carter Buschardt, Erv Karwelis and Idol Records, Barry and Teresa Beard, Vicky Williams, Lady Kunkle, Mike Rabon, Vivian Thompson, Sean Mitchell, James Goode, Kenny Daniel, Ty Grimes, John Lomax III, John Slate, Ruby Campbell, Cecil Cotten, Krum (TX) Museum, Whit Snell, Ron Dilulio, Kirby Warnock, B. J. Hardesty, Billy Lawson, Janice Ivey, Kathie May Hejny, Jamie Bassett, Jimmie Randall, Alan Struble, Mark Hamilton, Jay Taylor, Mark Ramsey, Gloria Wilkes, Dennis Recla, Barry Gremillion, David Faulkner, Judy Blundell, Jimmy McLellan, Erin Arthur, Mike Neal, T. Tex Edwards, Tom Huckabee, Ron Dyer, Christian Williams, James Ferris, Homer Henderson, Michelle Dudley, David Bullock, Freddie Cisneros, Hank Hankshaw, John Allen, Red Steagall, Casey Monahan, Don and Kathy Edwards, Randy Erwin, Judy Jergins, Fred Dobbs, Richard Bowden, Art Greenhaw.

George Gimarc: champion of Texas Underground Music for the '70s to the '90s; music director for the radio station The Edge, KDGE, 94.5: archivist for the Texas Musicians Museum; Texas Radio Hall of Fame inductee; and Grammy award winner. Courtesy of George Gimarc.

Musician and researcher Kevin Coffey (right) is shown here during his employment at Record Town in Fort Worth in the early 1990s with store cofounder Kathleen Bruton and her son, blue-chip bluesman Sumter Bruton. A frequent contributor to scholarly journals and deeply researched reissue liner notes, Coffey may know more than anyone about the history of western swing. Photo by Pete Kendall. Courtesy of Sumter Bruton / Record Town.

In addition to his work as a musician with The Novas and many other bands, David Dennard has provided valuable archival services with his research on the *Big "D" Jamboree* and the reissuing of *Jamboree* music on his own Dragon Street Records and on Bear Family Records. On January 2, 2003, David and William Williams started an Internet group, BigD60s, to research and archive the history of Dallas-Fort Worth music, focusing especially on the 1960s. Reuniting veterans of the North Texas sixties music scene, the group inspired and organized a number of Sixties Reunions, where many of the region's primary sixties bands made music together once again. This book in large part is the culmination of the research, archival efforts, and networking that began with BigD60s—a celebration of a rich musical tradition and heritage, of which we are fortunate to be a part. Courtesy of David Dennard.

Courtesy of the original Nevada Slim.

Index

C

F

G

N

O

X

Y

Z